Ribbons
and flowers

FLORISTS' REVIEW

~and~

FLORISTS' REVIEW

President: Frances Dudley, AAF

Publisher: Talmage McLaurin, AIFD

Authors: Carol Caggiano, AIFD, PFCI
Amy Bauer

Designers: Carol Caggiano, AIFD, PFCI
Talmage McLaurin, AIFD

Creative Coordinator: James Miller, AIFD

Copy Editors: David L. Coake
Kelsey E. Smith

Art Director: Holly Cott

Photographer: Stephen Smith

Ribbon products courtesy of: Berwick Offray LLC, *www.berwickindustries.com*
Lion Ribbon, *www.lionribbon.com*

Fresh flowers and foliages courtesy of: CallaCo; Moss Landing, Calif.; *www.callaco.com*
Eufloria Flowers; Nipomo, Calif.; *www.eufloriaflowers.com*
Ocean View Flowers; Lompoc, Calif.; *www.oceanviewflowers.com*
The Sun Valley Group; Arcata, Calif.; *www.tsvg.com*
Transflora; Miami, Fla.; *www.transflora.net*

Ribbons and Flowers was produced by Florists' Review Enterprises, Inc.
Topeka, Kansas USA; *www.floristsreview.com*

Printed by Inland Graphics, Menomonee Falls, Wisconsin USA

ISBN: 978-0-9801815-1-7

Florists' Review Enterprises is the leading magazine and book publishing company for the U.S. floral industry. The company is home to *Florists' Review* and *Super Floral Retailing* magazines as well as to Florists' Review Bookstore, the industry's premier marketplace for books and other educational materials.

When most of us think of *ribbon*, we envision beautifully wrapped gifts, little girls with precious bows in their hair, or maybe a majestic "blue ribbon" signifying the triumphant end of a challenge.

Ribbon has been used for centuries to decorate, adorn and celebrate every aspect of our lives. Today, the limitless array of fabrics, patterns, colors, textures and widths in which ribbon is available inspires innovation and creativity.

On these pages, we have combined ribbon with *flowers*, presenting our favorite design ideas and techniques in a how-to format, with the goals of encouraging you to re-create these designs or inspiring you to craft your own unique interpretations.

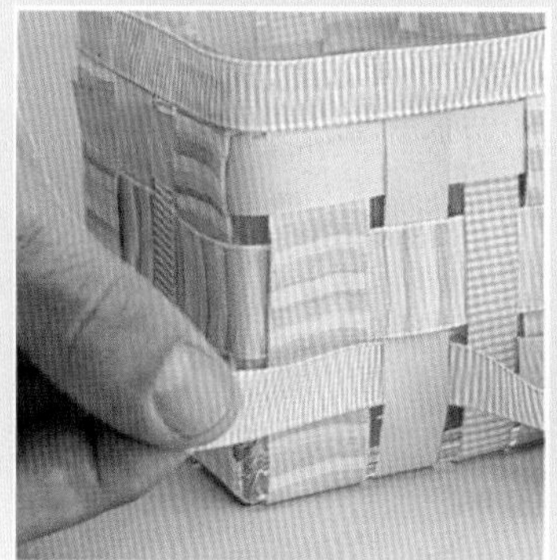

With ribbon, you will discover how easy and joyful it is to infuse your favorite floral projects with personality, style, texture, color, rhythm, emphasis and so much more. You will feel like a wizard of creativity, as the lengths of ribbon pass through your fingers, bringing a new dimension to every one of your designs.

Flipping through these pages, you will find *"inspiration by the yard"* and discover the magical versatility of ribbon.

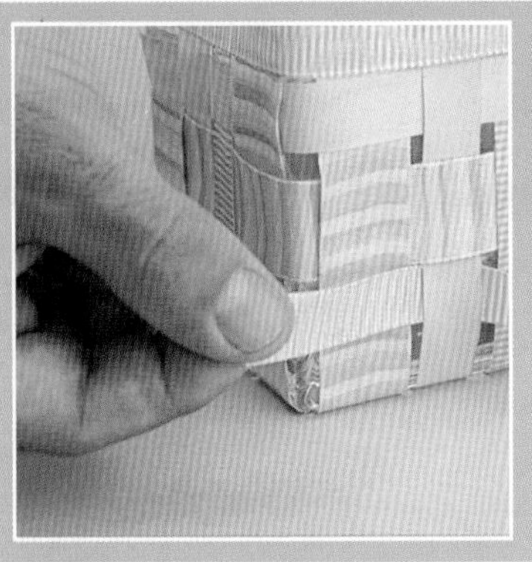

the arrival of spring fosters a renewal of creative spirit that can manifest in delightful design projects for the many special holidays and events of the season as well as everyday life.

(spring)

flight of fancy

*kid-friendly project

novelty ribbons cry out for creative applications, like this pair of glittering butterflies alighting among the dainty blossoms of a basketed *Kalanchoe* plant. A shimmery plaid ribbon trims the basket, along with a bow of beaded wire. Quick to create, these insect embellishments can enliven not only plants but also packages, napkins, wreaths, Christmas trees or wherever imagination calls.

how-to: ribbon butterfly

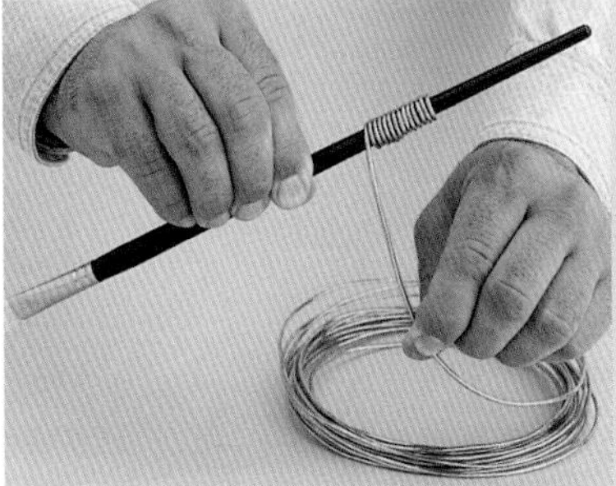

1) Coil decorative aluminum wire around a tapered paintbrush handle to create the butterfly's thorax (central body). Slip the wire coil off the handle.

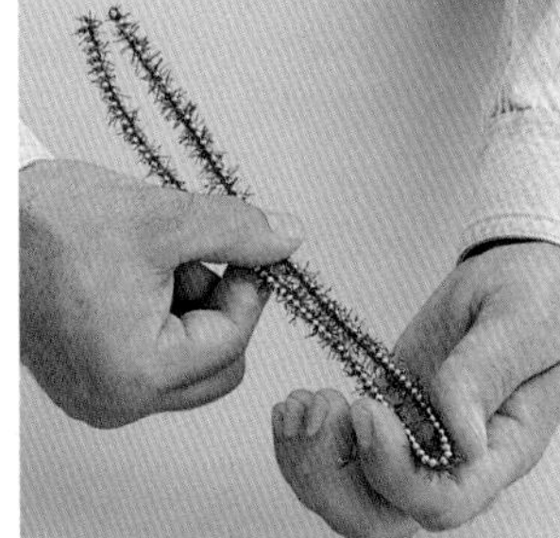

2) Fold a length of decorative beaded wire in half. This will create the butterfly's antennae and abdomen.

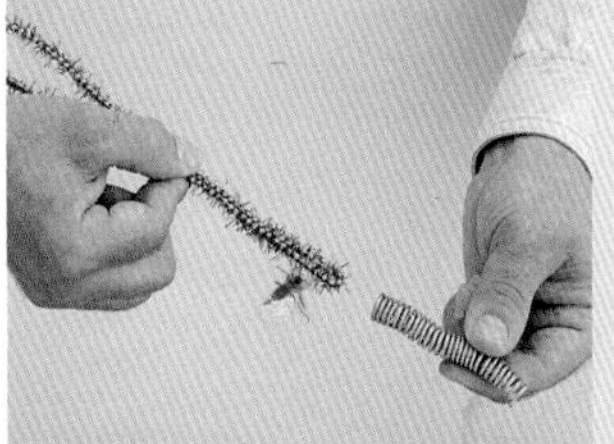

3) Slip the beaded wire into the wire coil made in Step 1.

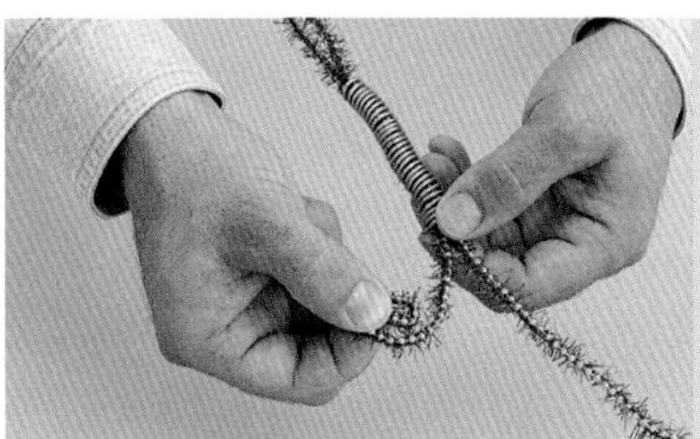

4) Coil the tips of the beaded wire to form the antennae.

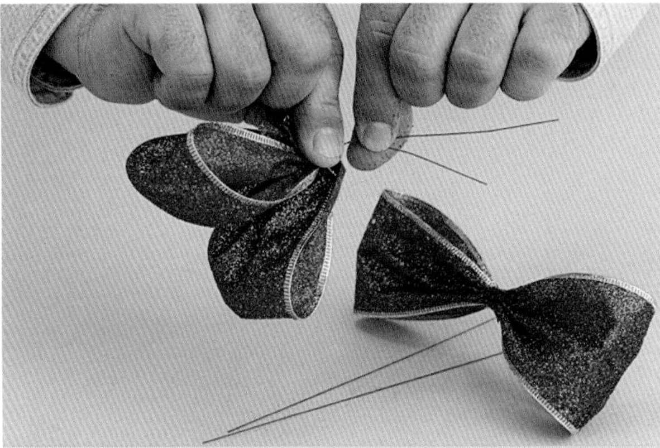

5) Make a pair of two-loop bows with 2½-inch-wide wire-edge sparkle ribbon, leaving no streamers. Make one bow larger than the other. With the larger bow on top, wire the two bows together to form wings. Tuck in the edges of the bows' loops to shape the wings.

6) Adhere the "body" atop the wings with hot glue. Gently shape the body to give form to the butterfly. Wire the butterflies to wood picks, and insert the picks into the soil of a plant.

miniature *maypole*

miniature maypole

Grosgrain ribbons, in *candy-colored* hot pinks and oranges and in various widths, stream from this flowery topiary to give the illusion of a blooming maypole. The ribbons' polka-dot and stitch patterns add youthful playfulness. There's no need to be exact; the differing lengths and widths of ribbon keep the presentation informal and fun. Bows add fullness to the mass of permanent flowers.

how-to: topiary form

1) Fill a ceramic pot with dry-floral foam or plastic foam, and cover the foam with moss. Dip one end of a branch into hot-melt (pan) glue, and insert it into the foam to form the topiary's stem. Apply hot glue to the top of the branch, and press a plastic-foam ball onto it.

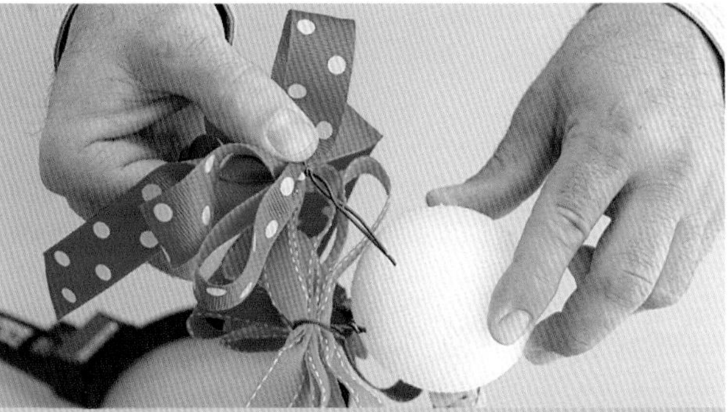

2) Make several small multiloop bows in various colors and patterns and in ⅜-inch, ⅝-inch and ⅞-inch widths. Tie the bows with short lengths of enameled florist's wire. Attach the bows to the plastic-foam ball by dipping the ends of the wire into hot-melt (pan) glue and inserting them into the foam ball.

3) Create ribbon streamers, and attach them to short lengths of wire. Dip the ends of the wire into hot-melt (pan) glue, and insert them into the base of the foam ball. Hot-glue permanent flowers among the bows and streamers to fill in spaces and create the floral design.

4) Trim the ends of the ribbon streamers with diagonal cuts.

gift with *fanfare*

stylish packaging makes a great first impression, and a little finesse turns an everyday present into an extraordinary presentation. Double-sided ribbon, in a contemporary stripe pattern, beautifully accents the vibrant lime-colored paper and creates a base for the permanent *Alstroemeria*, *Ranunculus* and *Viburnum* blossoms. Folded ribbon fans add showy appeal.

how-to: folded ribbon fans

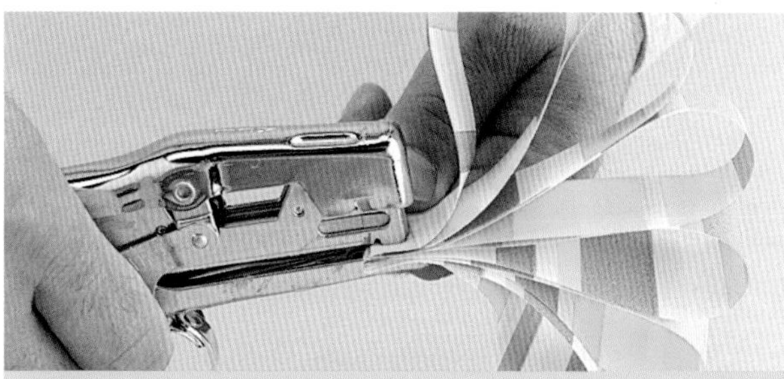

1) Form several contiguous loops with 1½-inch-wide ribbon (polypropylene and acetate satin work best). Staple the ribbon at the base of the loops.

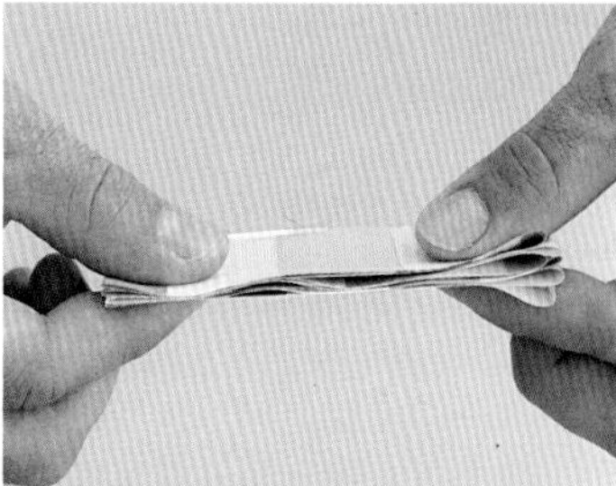

2) Flatten the other end of the loops, making perpendicular creases, to create a "pleated fan."

3) Wrap the package(s) with paper, and tie with ribbon, forming a two-loop "shoestring" bow on top of the package(s). Arrange permanent flowers into the bow, securing them in place with hot-melt (pan) glue.

Note: Fresh flowers also can be used. Liquid floral adhesive is recommended to affix them.

4) Place two or more pleated ribbon fans into openings among the cluster of blossoms, securing the fans in place with hot-melt (pan) glue.

sunny chandelier

Suspend this wreath horizontally to *set the mood* for a party or wedding, or in a kitchen or dining area to capture the season's bounty. A simple wire wreath form is hung upside down to cradle the permanent apples, sunflowers and *Viburnums*. Coordinating ribbons in solids and polka-dot and stitch patterns play up the bold sunflowers, and the generous use of streamers adds to the abundance.

how-to: hanging wreath

1) Spray-paint a wire wreath form the desired color with floral or enamel paint.

2) Tie lengths of ⅝-inch-wide ribbon in four evenly spaced places on the wire wreath form, and gather and tie the ends to form a hanger of a desired length. Add streamers, if desired, to the top, where the suspension ribbons are tied.

3) Create bows with ⅝-inch-wide and 1-inch-wide ribbons, and wire them onto the wire wreath form.

Note: Coordinating patterns of ribbon add interest.

4) Attach permanent fruit and flowers to the wire wreath form with hot-melt (pan) glue.

french fashion

Clear glass cylinder vases take on a *flirty*, feminine quality with the addition of a French-braid ribbon wrap, shown created in two ways. The tailored effect adds style to the inexpensive vases, and they are great to give as personalized gifts or to decorate for parties. Hot-pink ribbons with black-and-white accents are fashion-forward choices, but try other color pairings, as well.

how-to: shoestring bow

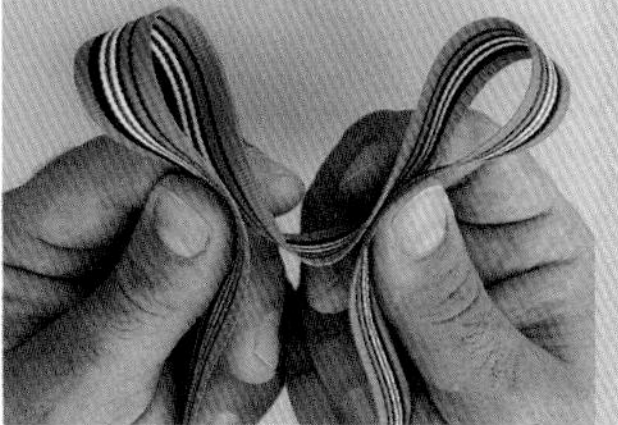

1) Holding a length of ⅞-inch-wide ribbon, create two loops.

2) Tie a two-loop bow by laying the left loop behind the right loop and laying the right loop over the left loop. Next, fold the top loop (the former right loop), over the bottom loop (the former left loop) and pull that loop through the opening in the lower center of the ribbon created by the original crossing of the loops.

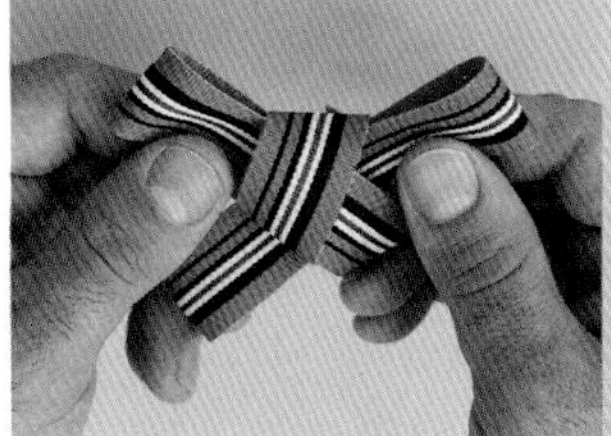

3) Holding both loops firmly, pull the bow tight, and adjust as needed. Cut inverted "V" patterns (a.k.a. dovetail or chevron cuts) into the ribbon ends.

4) Create several of these bows, and hot-glue them, at each ribbon twist, to a vase embellished with French-braided ribbon *(see Step 1 of adjacent How-To).*

how-to: french braid

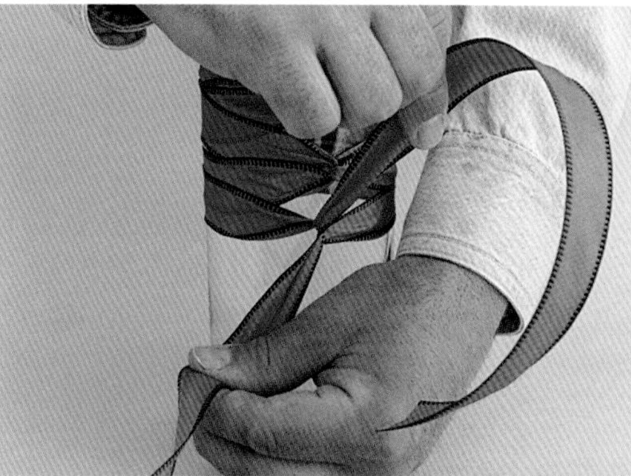

1) Hot-glue the center of a ⅞-inch-wide length of ribbon to a spot on the "backside" top of a cylinder vase, just below the rim. Bring the two ends of the ribbon forward, around the base (to the "front"), overlap the two ends, twist each end 180 degrees around the other end, and return each end back around the vase in the direction it came from. Pass the ends of ribbon over each other in the back of the vase, making sure they stay flat and smooth, and bring them around to the front of the vase again, where you repeat the twist.

Note: In this design, the twisting of the ribbon, which creates the braided look, is done on only one side of the vase.

Continue this procedure until you reach the bottom of the vase. Knot the ribbon at the bottom of the vase, in the front, to hold it in place.

2) Tie a four-loop bow into the knot. Cut inverted "V" patterns (a.k.a. dovetail or chevron cuts) into the ribbon ends.

patterns at *play*

coordinating striped and plaid ribbons, in a trio of spring hues, add modern charm to a classic table setting. A mass of simple two-loop bows dresses up a princess basket filled with seasonal flowers, including fragrant hyacinths and *Freesias*, *Viburnums*, *Hydrangeas*, *Lisianthuses* and tulips. And monobotanical accompaniments featuring the same flowers and ribbons make great party favors.

how-to: beribboned pot

Wrap 1½-inch-wide ribbon around the rim of a painted clay pot, and tie a knot. Cut inverted "V" patterns (a.k.a. dovetail or chevron cuts) into the ribbon ends.

how-to: ribbon-wrapped water tube

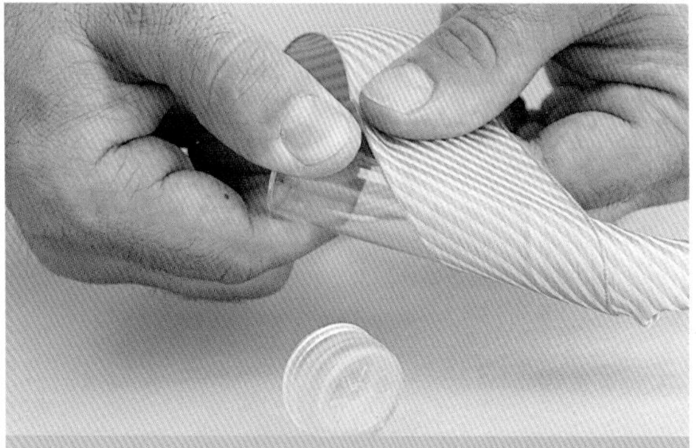

Lay a piece of ribbon along the bottom 1 inch or so of a water tube, parallel to the tube. Wrap the ribbon under the bottom of the tube, then begin wrapping the ribbon upward around the tube in an overlapping spiral manner. Secure the ribbon at the top of the tube with hot glue. Cap the tube, and tie a two-loop "shoestring" bow around the cap with a separate piece of ribbon to finish.

how-to: basket handle enhancement

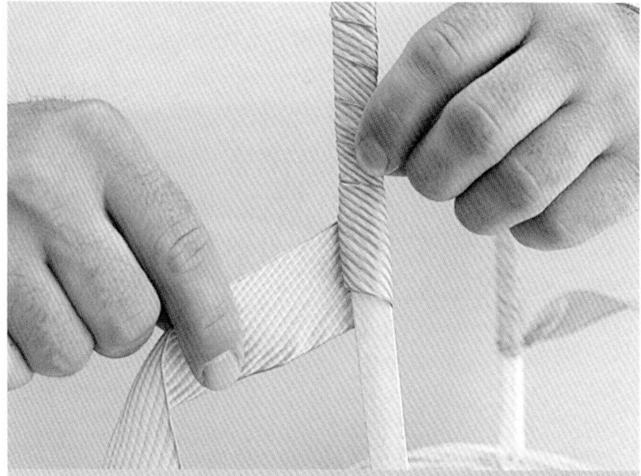

1) Tie an end of 1½-inch-wide ribbon into a knot at the base of one side of the basket handle. Begin wrapping the handle with the ribbon, tightly overlapping the ribbon, until the entire handle is covered. Secure the ribbon, again with a knot, at the base of the opposite side of the basket handle. Trim the ribbon ends with diagonal cuts.

2) Tie several lengths of coordinating patterns of 1½-inch-wide ribbon into two-loop "shoestring" bows around both handle bases, positioning the bows close together to give the illusion of a single bow. Trim the ribbon ends with diagonal cuts.

catch of the day

catch of the day

*kid-friendly project

Lilies, tulips and *Viburnums* take a whimsical *twist* with the addition of a river-cane pole and dangling glittered fish. Another sparkly fish appears to swim in the flower-filled bubble bowl, and coils of blue and yellow curling ribbons mimic a pond's ripples. Use this quick creation as a party theme, as a gift for Father's Day, or to surprise an outdoor lover or anyone in need of a smile.

how-to: ribbon fish

1) Adhere two lengths of 2½-inch-wide sparkle ribbon back to back with spray adhesive.

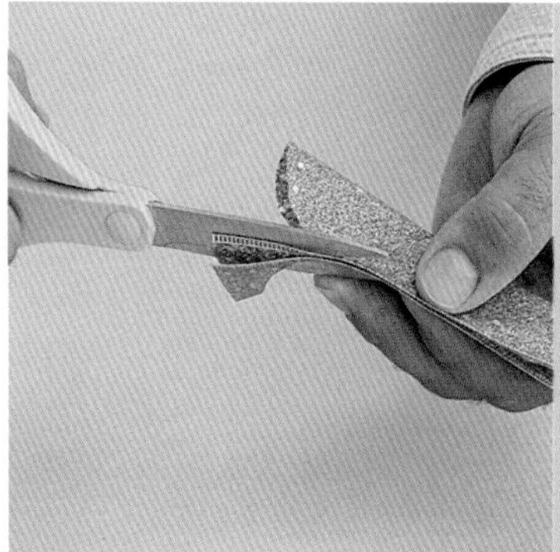

2) Fold the now double-faced ribbon in half lengthwise, and cut out a half-fish shape, using the fold as the center. When unfolded, the fish will be symmetrical, lengthwise.

3) Create an "eye" with a hole punch. Tie monofilament through the eye hole, and suspend the fish from the pole.

4) Run lengths of curling ribbon over a knife or scissors blade to curl. *(Note: Make sure the back of the ribbon is against the blade.)* Tuck the ribbon curls into the vases to create interest in the water, and submerge a ribbon fish into the bubble bowl.

hippie chic

hippie *chic*

*kid-friendly project

Festive, *happy gerberas*, tied with psychedelic solid and striped ribbons, impart a bohemian aesthetic to a novel centerpiece and ready-to-go favors ideal for a birthday party or shower. The vase, too, is embellished with ribbons. Tying ribbons to the flower stems ensures a lush look and that each guest leaves with a floral gift. Experiment with other ribbon colors and patterns to create different moods.

how-to: beribboned blooms and vase

1) Attach lengths of ⅞-inch-wide and 1½-inch-wide ribbons to the rim of a vase with hot glue. Let streamers drape onto the table, trimming the ends with diagonal cuts.

2) Hot-glue a band of ribbon to encircle the rim and cover the ribbon ends.

3) Tie ribbons to the *Gerbera* stems, just beneath the flower heads, using one, two or three coordinating patterns on each stem. Leave the streamers long enough to also drape onto the table.

4) Arrange the *Gerberas* into the vase, allowing the ribbon streamers to drape gracefully outside the vase. Trim the ends of the streamers with diagonal cuts.

natural *glamour*

Glittering ribbon *roses and leaves* add sparkle to spring in this inventive nested topiary in fashion-forward teal and brown hues. Coordinating ribbons swirl through the ready-made nest and anchor the roses with loops and streamers picked into the foam inside a sweet ceramic pot. Miniature permanent blossoms add a floral accompaniment.

how-to: ribbon rose

1) Holding a length of 2½-inch-wide wire-edge sparkle ribbon horizontally, fold the right end toward you, down and perpendicular to the ribbon, forming a 90-degree angle.

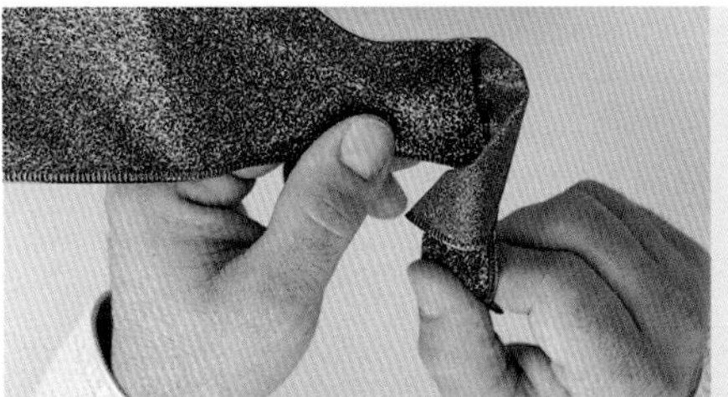

2) Tightly roll the folded-down section of the ribbon, from right to left, until you reach the end of the folded portion.

3) In a manner similar to the process described in Step 1, fold the next section of ribbon down and perpendicular to the length of ribbon, but this time fold it underneath (behind, or away from you instead of toward you).

4) Continue to roll the folded-down section of ribbon to the left, angling along the fold and stopping when the end of the folded portion is reached. Repeat Step 3 and this step until the rose reaches the desired size. Secure the rose's shape by tightly binding the two ribbon ends with florist's wire at the base of the flower.

how-to: ribbon leaf

1) To create ribbon leaves, fold a section of ribbon in half lengthwise, and cut out a half-leaf shape, with the fold serving as the center of the leaf. When the ribbon is unfolded, both sides of the leaf shape will be the same.

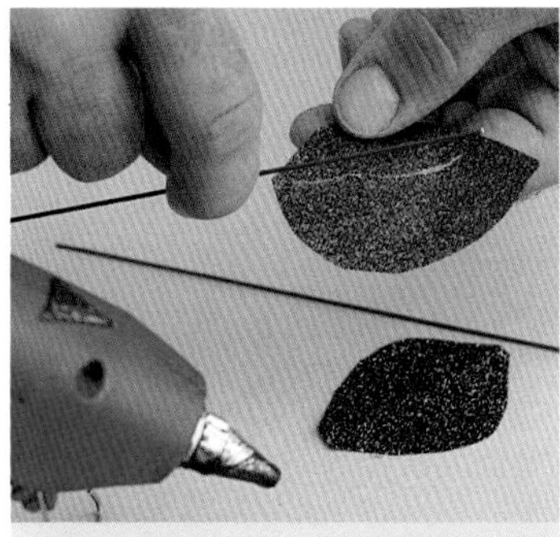

2) Hot-glue a piece of florist's wire to the back of each leaf. Form the leaves into lifelike shapes.

clever cubes

b.

c.

a.

Whether used singly to *accent small spaces* or arranged as a composite centerpiece, these cube vases are clever imposters. A trio of coordinating ribbons creates the look of a woven basket and perfectly tied packages. And the ribbon ties over the opening of the center cube help hold the flowers in place. While this pastel color combination makes a sweet statement, bolder hues can alter the look.

a. how-to: basket weave

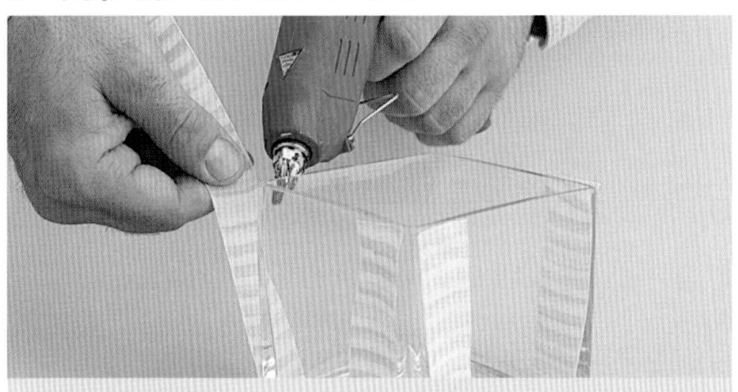

1) Beginning at the rim on one side of a square glass vase, attach a length of 1-inch-wide ribbon to the outside of the vase with hot glue. Pull the ribbon underneath the vase, adhering it again at the opposite rim. Glue only the ends of each strip. Repeat this procedure around the vase, using coordinating ribbon patterns and a combination of ⅝-inch and 1-inch widths.

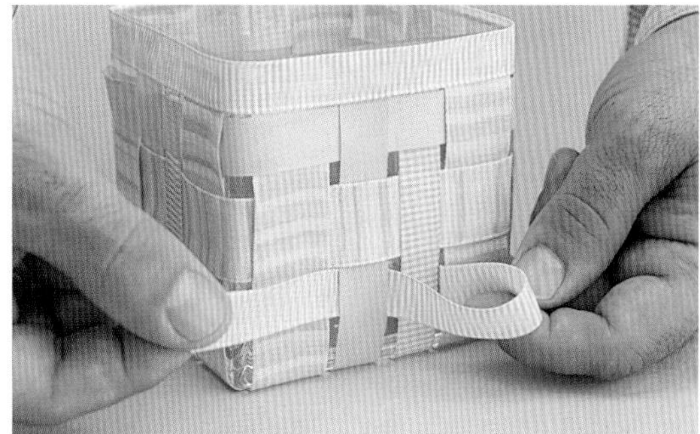

2) Weave lengths of ribbon horizontally through the vertical ribbons, attaching the ends with hot glue. Be sure to alternate the over-and-under pattern on each row to create a basket weave. Finish the top edge by hot-gluing a band of ribbon around the rim of the vase.

b. how-to: package wrap

1) Holding one end of a length of 1-inch-wide ribbon in place along one side of a square glass vase, wrap the ribbon over the opening of the vase, down the opposite side of the vase, underneath the vase, and up the side of the vase on which you began. Pass the ribbon over the center of the opening of the vase, and cross the ribbon ends and twist them 90 degrees. Next, repeat the ribbon-wrapping process on the opposite sides of the vase. Tie the ribbon ends into a knot over the opening of the vase.

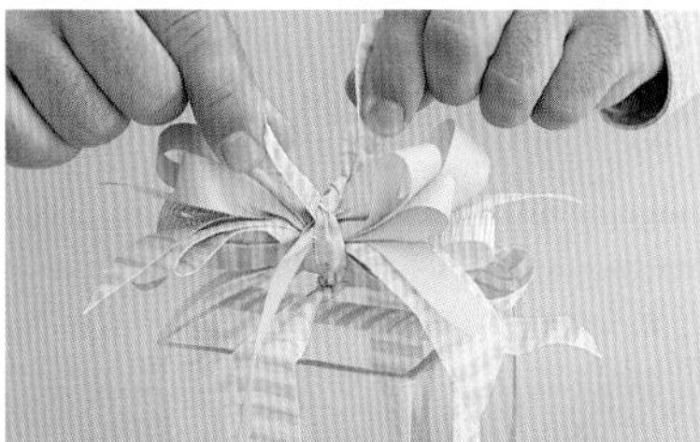

2) Tie loops of various patterns and widths of ribbon into the knot to form a festive bow. Trim the ends of the ribbon with diagonal cuts. Arrange flowers into the vase, among the loops of ribbon.

c. how-to: bow-tie bow

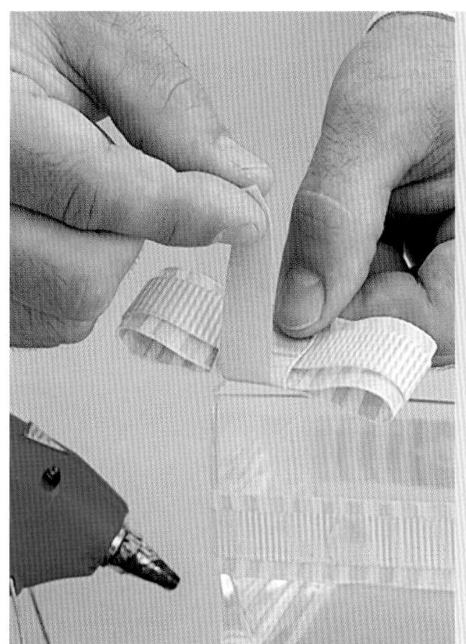

1) Hot-glue one end of a length of 1-inch-wide ribbon to the center of one side of a square glass vase. Wrap the ribbon horizontally around the mid-section of the vase, and secure the other end of the ribbon over the first with more hot glue. Adhere a second ribbon, in a coordinating pattern and a narrower width (⅝ inch shown), over the wider ribbon, in the same manner. Create a two-loop Dior-style bow from the two patterns and widths of ribbon, and secure it in the center with a staple. Wrap a length of contrasting ribbon around the center to cover the staple, and adhere it in back with hot glue. Attach the bow to the horizontal ribbon band on the vase with hot glue, covering the overlapped ends.

2) Arrange flowers into the vase, and using the eraser end of a pencil, tuck a continuous length of ribbon between blooms. Create full loops so they show nicely among the blossoms.

custom *candlescape*

enhance any décor by upgrading glass containers with an array of like-hued ribbons. In addition to the varied ribbon edgings, sparkly gemstones spice up the vases. A floral-foam wreath form, bedecked with fragrant star-shaped *Stephanotises*, *Berzelia*, and *Pittosporum* and *Camellia* foliage, encircles the central cylinder, which serves as a holder for a pillar candle. A *Gardenia* floats in another cylinder.

how-to: ribbon-edged containers

1) Encircle a glass cylinder container with 1½-inch-wide picot-edge ribbon, overlapping the ends of the ribbon. Holding the ribbon tightly, slip it off the cylinder.

2) Cut the ribbon at the overlap. This will create a length exactly right for the circumference of the cylinder. Measure and cut additional lengths of ribbon in the same manner, in a variety of patterns and widths (½-inch and 1½-inch widths are used in this example).

3) Spray adhesive onto the back of each length of ribbon, and press it onto the glass. Keep the ribbon taut so it stays flat and smooth as you press it on.

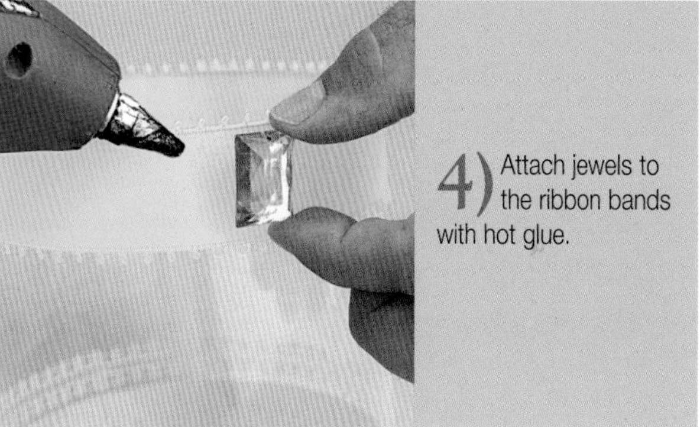

4) Attach jewels to the ribbon bands with hot glue.

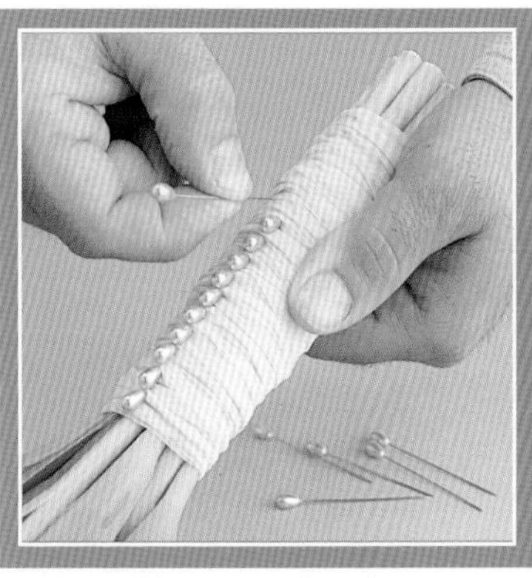

attention to detail is essential in creating harmonious décor for today's nuptial events. Ribbons and flowers join in blissful harmony in designs covering every aspect of weddings, from ceremony to reception.

(wedding)

ready to wear

Mixing *satin* and *sparkle* ribbons, along with a few sparkling jewels, into a stylish bow base creates a captivating corsage. Ribbon ties enhance the romantic flair. The bow base, which cushions and protects the spray roses, can be made ahead of time. Ribbon-wrapping and a coordinating jewel pick ensure a perfect match in the boutonniere.

how-to: corsage

1) Make two small 10-loop bows from ⅝-inch-wide sheer sparkle ribbon and one small 10-loop bow from ⅜-inch-wide double-face satin ribbon. Secure each bow with florist's wire. Gather the three bows to form one large bow, and twist their wires together. Cut away any excess wire.

2) Tie a length of the satin ribbon through the center of the bow, leaving streamers long enough to tie the corsage to the wrist when completed.

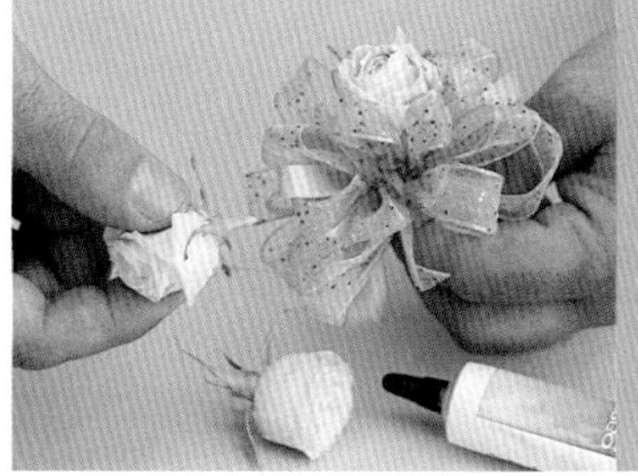

3) Glue flowers into the bow with liquid floral adhesive.

how-to: boutonniere

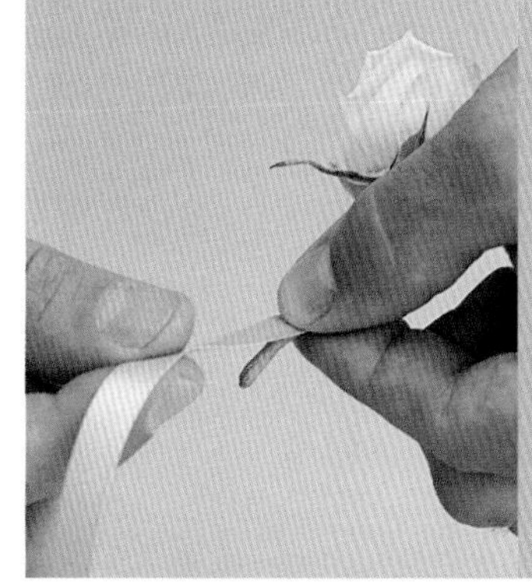

1) Hold a length of satin ribbon parallel to the flower stem, with the end of the ribbon toward the flower and about an inch of the ribbon covering the stem.

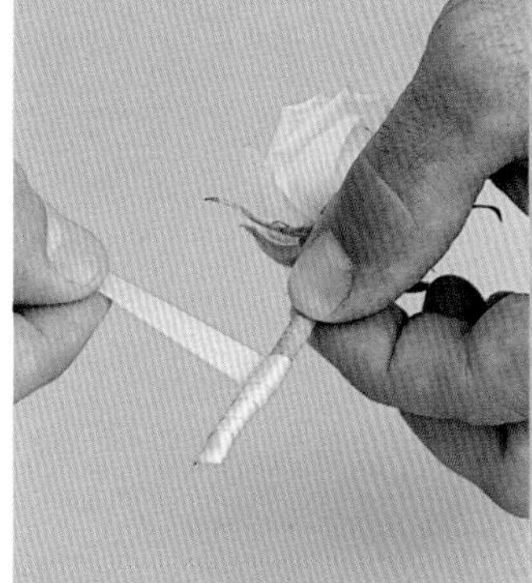

2) Begin wrapping the stem at the bottom, working upward toward the flower.

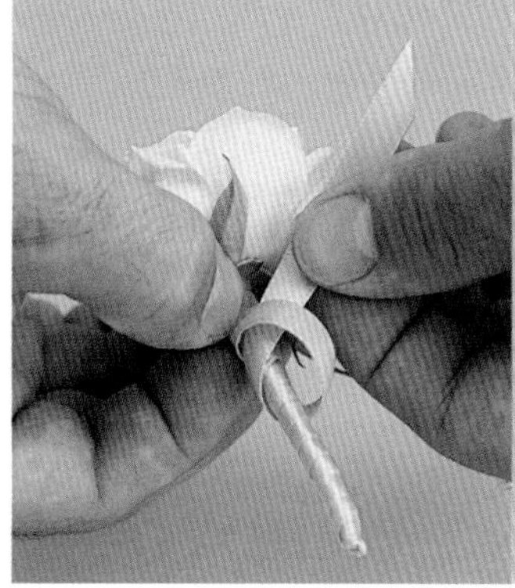

3) At the top of the stem, loop the ribbon and tuck the end through. Pull tight to secure. Leave a small streamer, and trim its end with a diagonal cut.

collar *quartet*

collar *quartet*

a.

b.

c.

d.

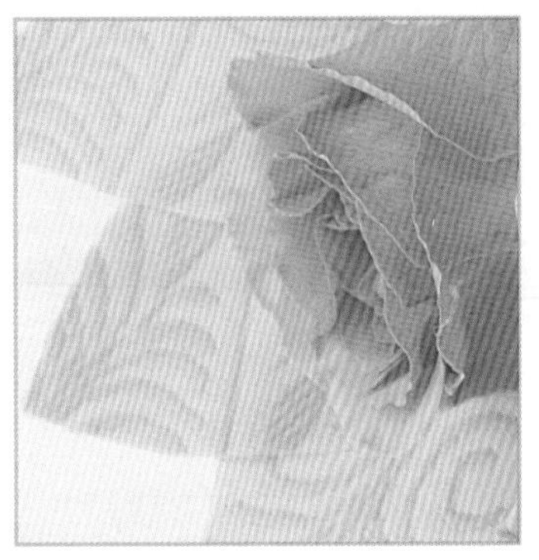

From lacy and *romantic* to sleek and *contemporary*, these four simple bouquet collar techniques make it easy to create a variety of moods. While these examples all are finished in creamy ivory, the ribbon color choices are endless. When colors to match a bride's scheme are difficult to find in nature, ribbons can assist. And these collars can be used with fresh or permanent blooms.

a. how-to: ribbon leaf collar

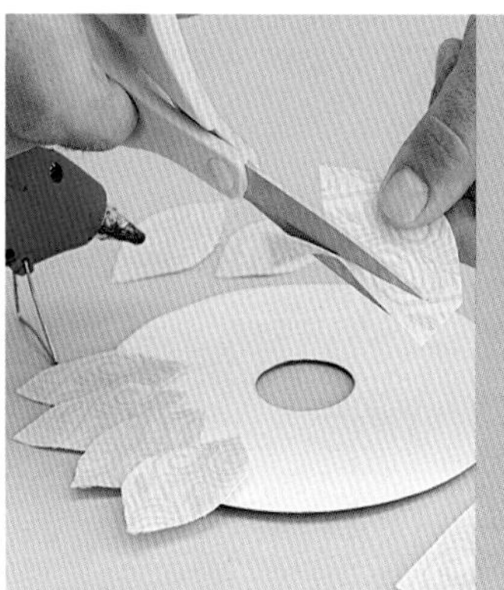

1) Cut a leaf shape from a 1½-inch-wide ribbon. *(Make sure the ribbon you select is fairly stiff.)* Use the first leaf as a pattern to create additional leaves. Adhere the leaves, with hot glue, around a piece of cardboard removed from a bolt of ribbon. Overlap the leaves slightly.

Note: If the desired diameter of cardboard isn't available, cut a circular piece of foam-centered board.

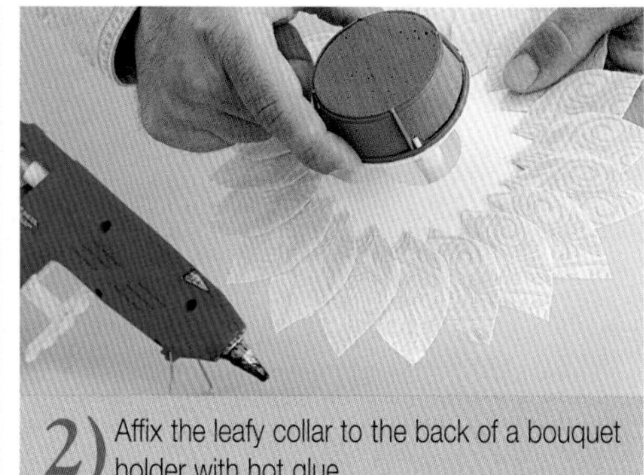

2) Affix the leafy collar to the back of a bouquet holder with hot glue.

b. how-to: lace bow collar

1) Make several four-loop bows from 2½-inch-wide lace ribbon, and secure the bows with florist's wire. Wire the bows to wood picks. Wrap the wood picks with stem wrap to prevent water from wicking into the lace bows from the bouquet holder.

2) Dip the wrapped wood picks into liquid floral adhesive, and insert them into a bouquet holder, around its perimeter, to form a ruffly, lacy collar.

c. how-to: ribbon loop collar

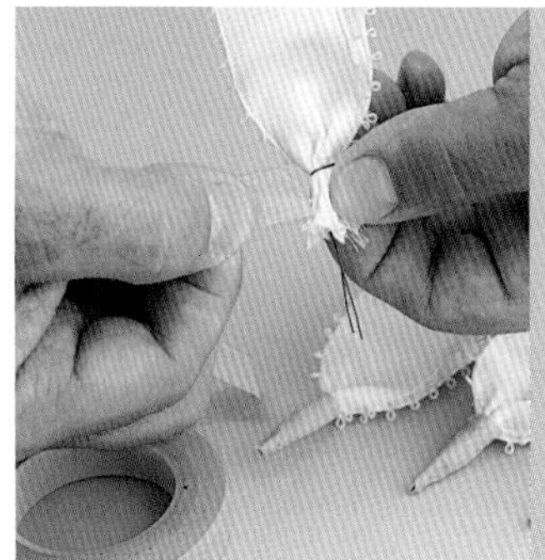

1) Create individual loops of 1½-inch-wide picot-edge ribbon, wiring the ends tightly with florist's wire. Wrap the base of the ribbon loops and the wire "stems" completely with stem wrap to ensure the ribbon won't wick water from the bouquet holder.

2) Dip the wrapped wire "stems" into liquid floral adhesive, and insert them into a bouquet holder, around its perimeter, to form a collar.

d. how-to: ribbon disc collar

1) Wrap 1½-inch-wide ribbon around a piece of cardboard removed from a bolt of ribbon, completely covering the cardboard. Pull the final wrap of ribbon through the center hole, leaving it long and securing it in place, to the cardboard, with a straight pin.

Note: If the desired diameter of cardboard isn't available, cut a circular piece of foam-centered board.

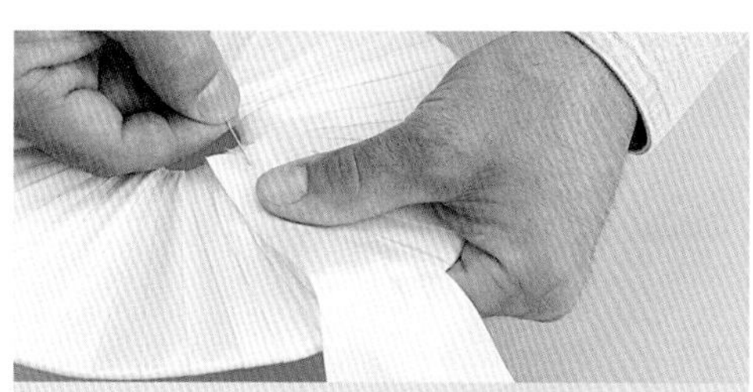

2) Secure a second streamer of the same length atop the first using another straight pin. Trim the streamer ends with diagonal cuts. Affix the collar to the back of a bouquet holder with hot glue.

chair-back *garland*

no shortcuts are evident in this opulent garland, though its creation saves the time involved in cutting and tying numerous individual bows. Continuous lengths of ribbon are looped and knotted to form a base for the roses and *Freesias*. The garland can adorn a chair back or be created in any length and color palette for church or reception-hall décor.

how-to: ribbon-and-flower swag

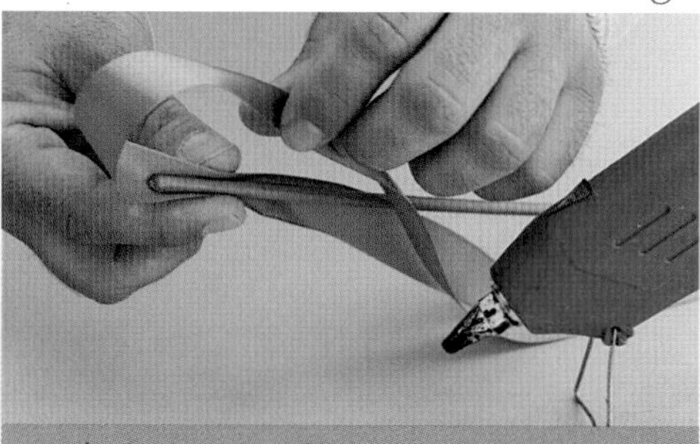

1) Glue a loop of ⅞-inch-wide ribbon to each end of a long permanent-flower stem (1½ times the width of the chair back). These loops are used to attach the finished decoration to the chair.

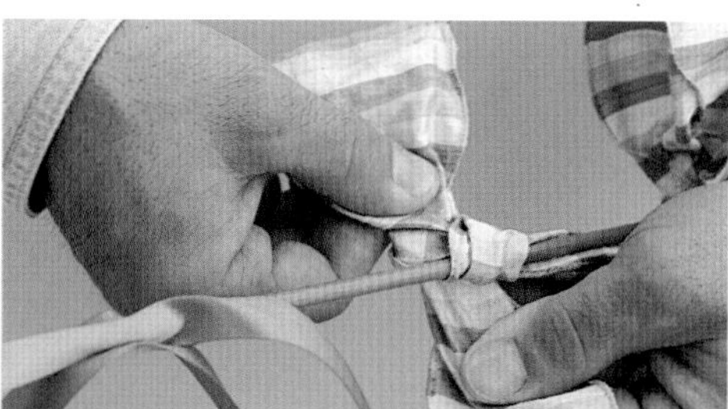

2) Tightly tie two-loop "shoestring" bows of a 2½-inch-wide patterned ribbon, along the flower stem, beginning at one end and working toward the other. Leave about 2 inches between bows.

3) Tie more two-loop "shoestring" bows of the next ribbon, a 5-inch-wide sheer, alongside the previously created bows. Repeat the process with the ⅞-inch-wide satin ribbon that was used to create the hanger loops, as well as a 6-inch-wide tulle. Continue with other patterns, colors and widths of ribbon, if desired.

Note: Combining tulle with sheer, silk and satin ribbons creates a rich look.

4) Glue fresh flowers into the ribbon base with liquid floral adhesive, tucking the blossoms among the ribbon loops.

Note: Pour an amount of the adhesive into a paint-can lid so you can quickly dip flower stems into it and arrange them among the ribbon loops.

toast-ready *roses*

toast-ready roses

atop the cake, a silk ribbon bow, made with the same ribbon that encircles the layers of the cake, is the base for the arrangement of ribbon roses and fresh *Stephanotises*. Additional ribbon roses embellish toasting glasses and a cake knife and server.

how-to: ribbon rose

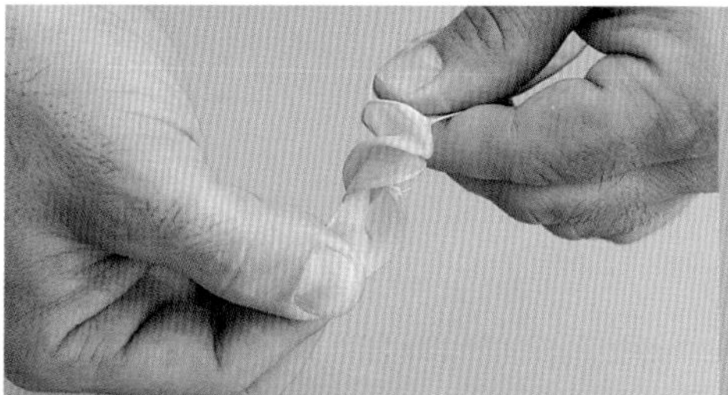

1) Knot one end of a 1½-inch-wide wire-edge ombre sheer ribbon. *Note: An ombre ribbon fades, from one edge to the other, from light to dark or from one color to another.*

2) At the opposite end of the length of ribbon, pull the wire on one edge, gathering the ribbon along the wire. Pulling the wire on the lighter-colored edge will create a darker rose and vice versa.

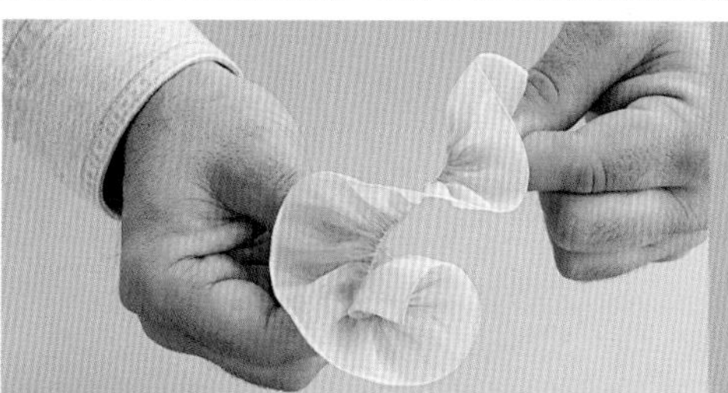

3) Holding the knot, wrap the gathered ribbon around it to form a rose.

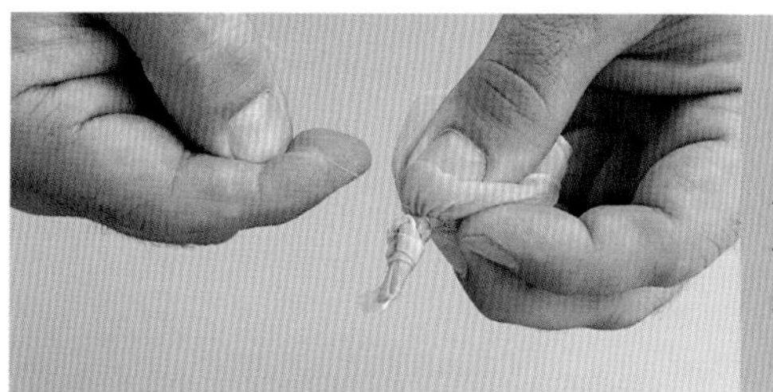

4) Once the rose is formed, wrap the wire tightly around the base of the flower, above the knot, to secure its shape.

how-to: cake topper

1) Make a four- or five-loop bow with 2½-inch-wide wire-edge ribbon. Tie the bow with a length of the same ribbon.

2) Fluff the bow, then crush it slightly to shape it into a semicircular form to use as the base for the cake topper. Glue in fabric and/or fresh flowers with liquid floral adhesive.

airy pomander

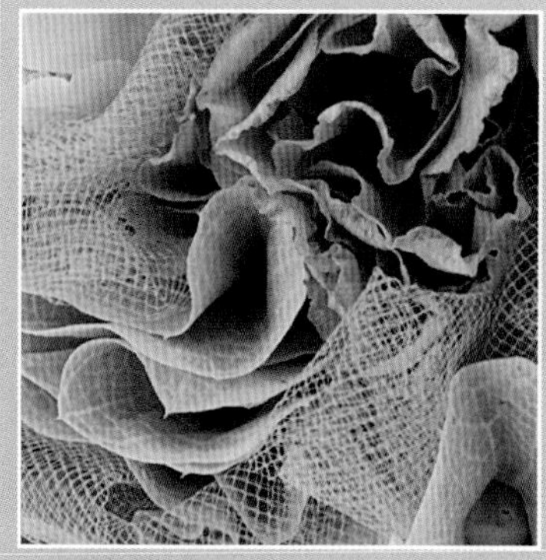

light as a feather, this tulle-based pomander bouquet is just right for the littlest flower girl or as a unique bouquet for a bridesmaid. Fresh roses, *Lisianthuses*, stocks and bells-of-Ireland are glued into the tulle, which cushions and protects them, but permanent blooms could be used, as well. Make the tulle bases well ahead to save time as the event nears.

how-to: bouquet handle and base

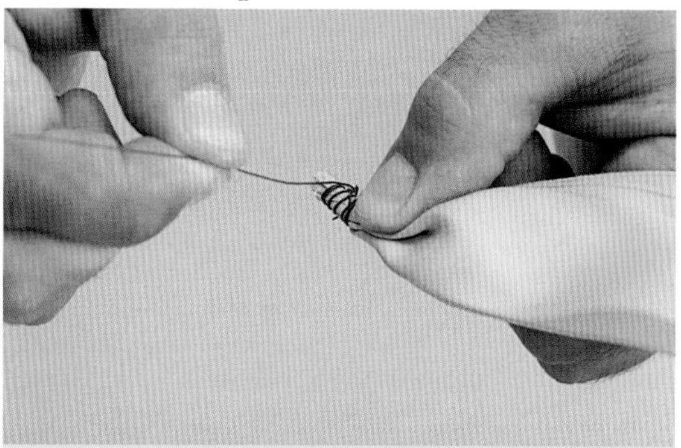

1) Bind together, at one end, three lengths of 1½-inch-wide ribbon with a piece of florist's wire.

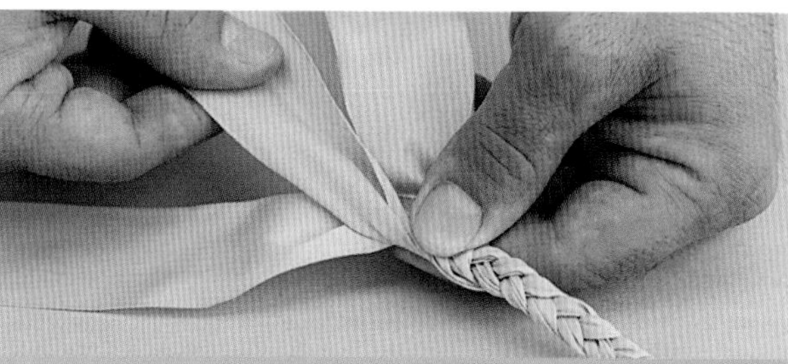

2) Braid the three ribbons using a traditional braiding technique: right ribbon pulled over center ribbon, then left ribbon pulled over center ribbon, then right, then left, and so on. *Note: Attach the bound end of the ribbon to something stationary so that you can keep the braid taut and even.*

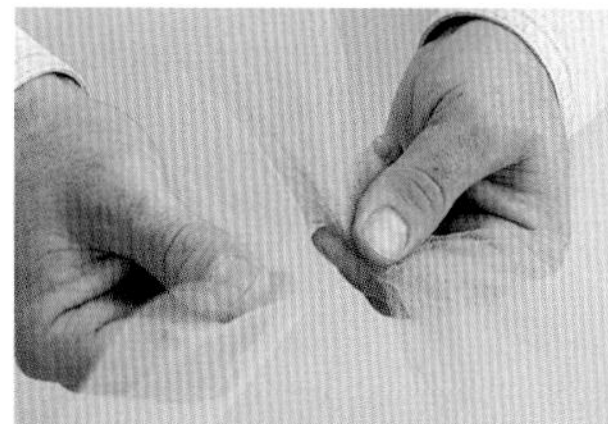

3) Create a full, multiple-loop bow from 6-inch-wide tulle. Keep the center tightly cinched.

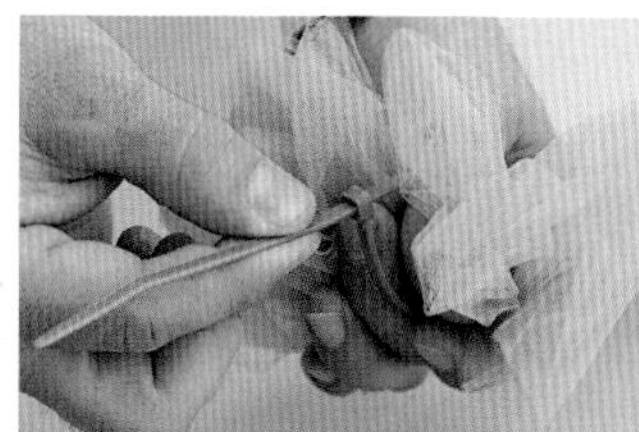

4) Bind the tulle bow tightly with a cable tie. Cut away the excess length of cable tie.

5) Create a loop with the braid made in Steps 1 and 2, binding the ends together with a cable tie. Tuck the fluffy tulle bow into the loop, and bind the braid again, just above the bow, with a third cable tie. Cut the excess lengths from both cable ties.

6) Fluff the tulle bow to create a round form. Glue in fresh, permanent and/or dried flowers with liquid floral adhesive. Finish by tying a two-loop "shoestring" bow with the same ribbon used for the braided handle, around the handle base, atop the bouquet.

retro rosette

A *nostalgic gift* can be enjoyed before the package is ever opened, with this paper "cummerbund" into which heirloom photos are tucked. A gray ribbon rosette and permanent leaves painted the same hue replace the traditional bow. A knotted width of peach-colored half-satin/half-sheer ribbon adds a touch of color to this stylish palette, perfectly in step with the black-and-white photos.

how-to: ribbon rose

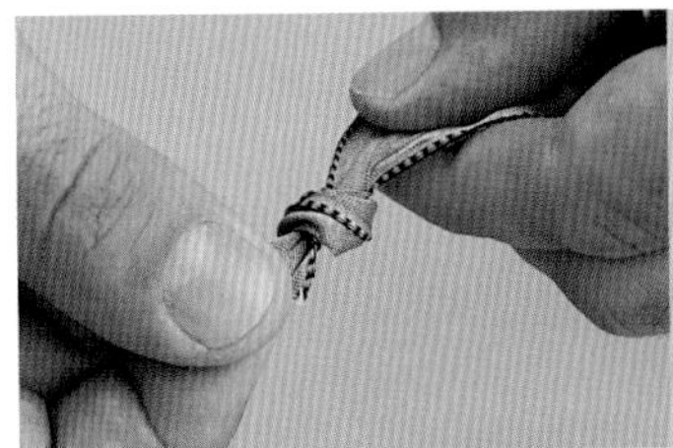

1) Knot the end of a 1½-inch-wide wire-edge ribbon.

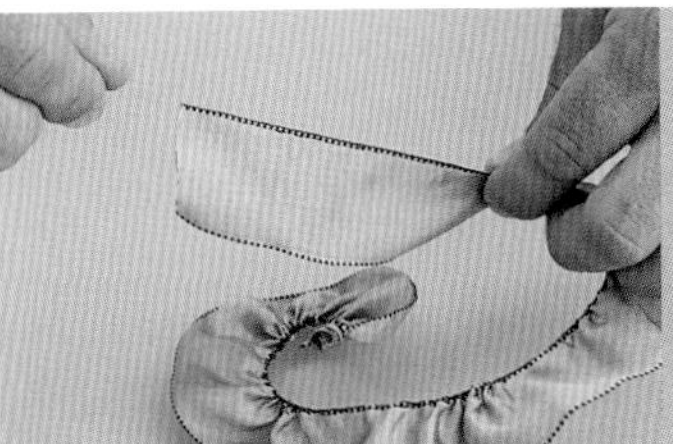

2) Pull one of the wires at the other end of the ribbon, and gather the ribbon along the wire.

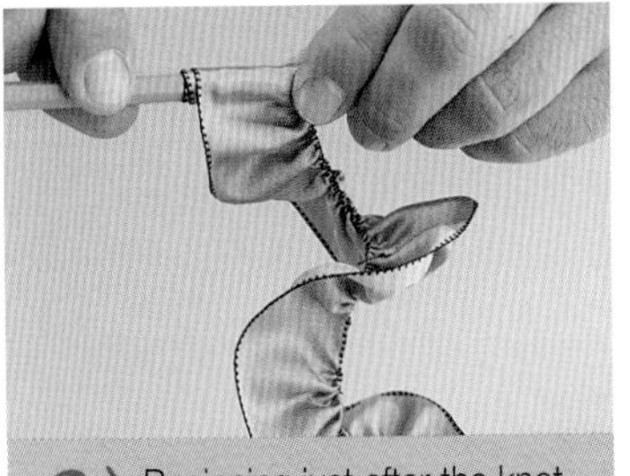

3) Beginning just after the knot, roll the ribbon around a pencil to create a tight center. Leave the knot alongside the pencil and below the roll.

4) Remove the pencil, and continue rolling the gathered ribbon around the center to form the rest of the rose. Wrap the pulled wire tightly around the base of the rose, above the knot, to secure the creation.

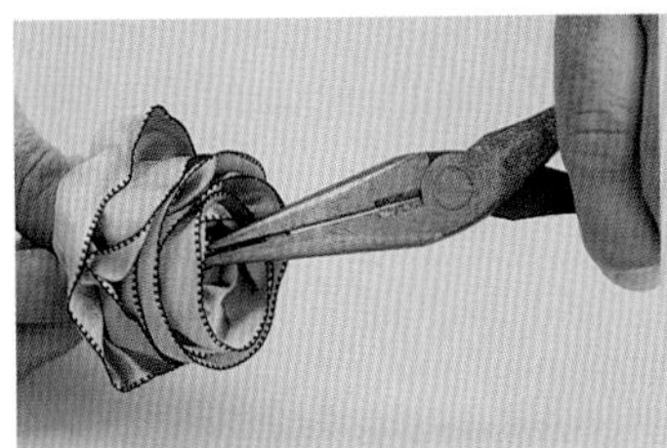

5) Grasp the center of the rose with needle-nose pliers, and twist to tighten.

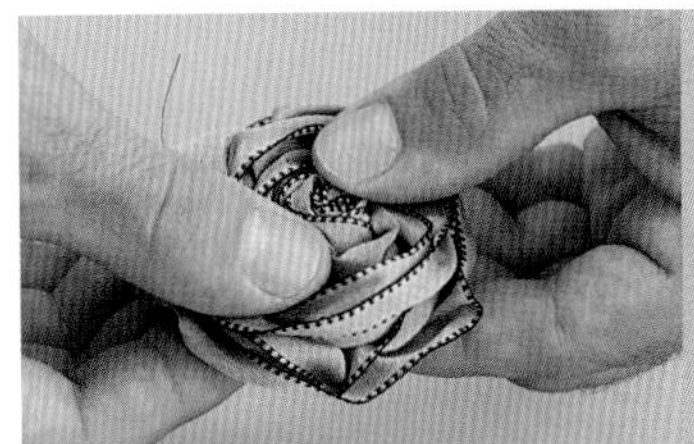

6) Flatten the rose, and mold to an attractive form.

belles of the ball

belles of the ball

Ball-gown-style ribbon "skirts" *dress up* arrangement containers for a bridal shower or luncheon. The pink-and-yellow plaid adds an old-fashioned aesthetic, as does the dusty-miller foliage. Varied ribbon widths allow for either multiple layering or accenting both small and large vessels. Any color scheme can be matched, and other ribbon types, such as eyelet or lace, also would be lovely.

how-to: ribbon skirts

1) Remove the wire from one edge of a length of 4-inch-wide wire-edge plaid ribbon.

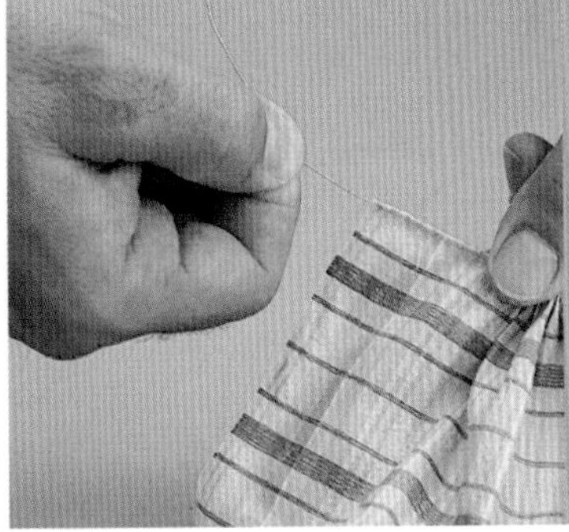

2) Crimp one end of the remaining wire to secure it in place. Holding the wire's other end, gather the ribbon along the wire to create a skirt-like effect.

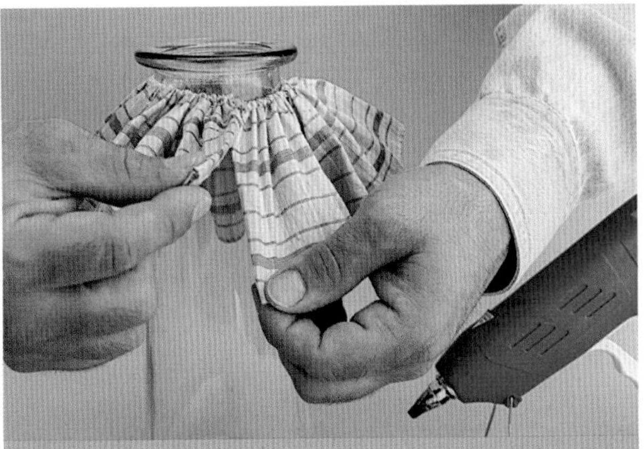

3) Glue the ribbon "skirt" around the neck or rim of the chosen container with hot glue, overlapping and gluing together the ends of the ribbon.

Note: Try layering "skirts" of coordinating ribbons for a full effect.

4) Encircle a ⅝-inch-wide ribbon around the rim of the container to cover the gathers, and tie it into a two-loop "shoestring" bow.

aisles of color

a.

b.

c.

d.

This quartet of colorful pew *adornments* shows the range of styles that can be created with various patterns and colors of ribbon and by altering the construction techniques slightly. The showy bows encourage simple monobotanical floral selections. Whether crafted for every pew or just a few key seats, these creations ensure an impressive aisle display.

a. *how-to:* ribbon "badge"

1) Create a loop and streamer from 4-inch-wide wire-edge ribbon. Repeat two times, making one streamer longer than the other two. Bind the three loop/streamer pieces together with florist's wire, with the longest streamer in the center. Repeat this process with a 3-inch-wide wire-edge ribbon, creating four smaller loop/streamer pieces. Wire these four loop/streamer pieces together, then wire them, as a unit, to the larger triple-loop/streamer set.

2) Fold both corners of every streamer backward, into the center of the streamer, to create a point. Hot-glue the corners in place on the backside of the streamers. Glue roses into the center of the ribbon "badge" with liquid floral adhesive.

b. *how-to:* bow with curled streamers

Create a 10-loop bow with multiple streamers from 2½-inch-wide wire-edge ribbon. Wire loops and streamers of a coordinating 1½-inch-wide patterned ribbon into the larger bow. Roll the streamers of the larger bow into coils, with a pencil. Cut inverted "V" patterns (a.k.a. dovetail or chevron cuts) into the ends of the patterned ribbon streamers. Tie this creation to the stems of a bunch of *Lisianthuses* with another length of ribbon.

c. *how-to:* multiple ribbon bow

Make a six-loop bow from a 2½-inch-wide wire-edge ribbon and a smaller six-loop bow from a 2-inch-wide wire-edge ribbon in a coordinating pattern or color. Wire the smaller bow into the center of the larger bow, to form a single bow. Glue *Hydrangeas* into the center with liquid floral adhesive.

d. *how-to:* rows of bows

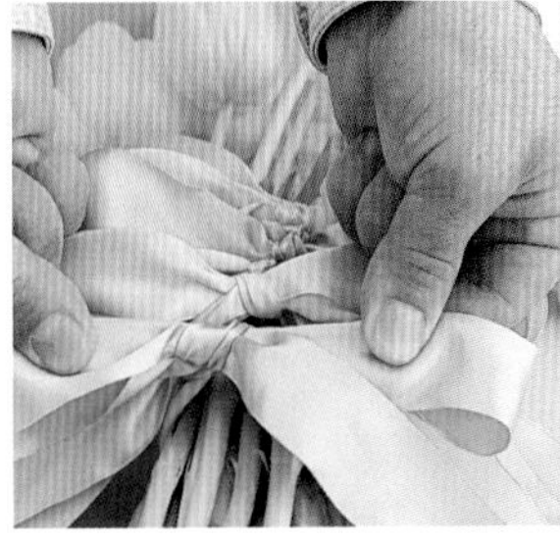

1) Tie successive two-loop "shoestring" bows, with long streamers, onto a bunch of tulip stems, beginning at the lowest point and working up the stems. Make all bows the same size, and tuck the streamers behind the preceding bows.

2) Thread a length of ribbon through a rhinestone buckle, and wrap the ribbon vertically over the centers of the bows to cover the knots. Tuck in the ribbon ends, and secure with boutonniere pins.

lasting *romance*

lasting romance

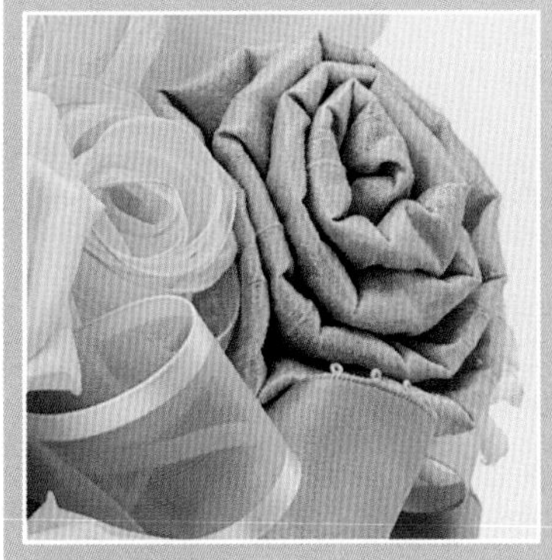

The *romance of a bygone era* is captured in this ribbon-rose shower bouquet, into which a few fresh roses are arranged. Bows and streamers in coordinating ribbon patterns make up the base, and novelty rosette ribbon adds a delicate finishing touch. The fabric flowers are a lasting keepsake and can be created in colors not easily found in fresh florals.

how-to: rose bouquet

1) Make five large six-loop bows from an assortment of ribbons, in a variety of colors and widths (⅝-inch, 1½-inch and 2¼-inch widths are shown here). These bows will form the base of the bouquet. Using stem wrap, tape the wires that secure the bows.

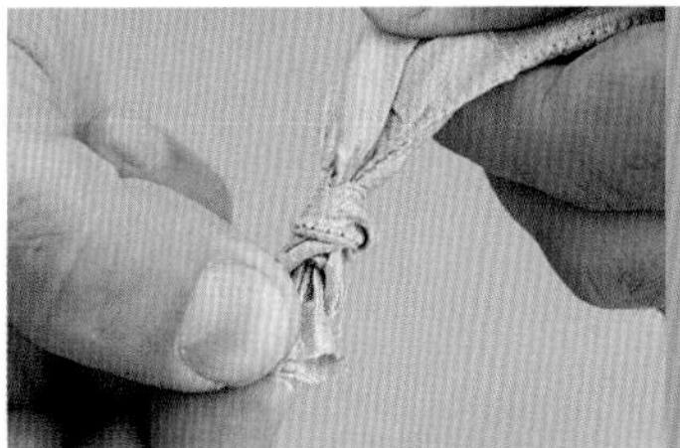

2) To make these ribbon roses, begin by tying a knot in the end of a 3-inch-wide wire-edge ribbon.

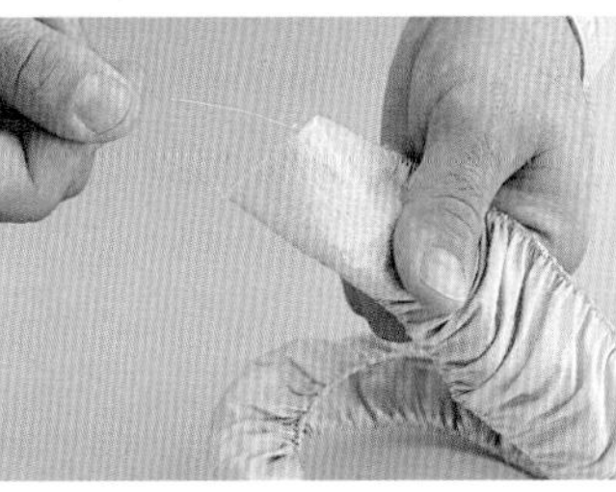

3) Pull on both wires at the opposite end of the ribbon, and gather the ribbon along the wires.

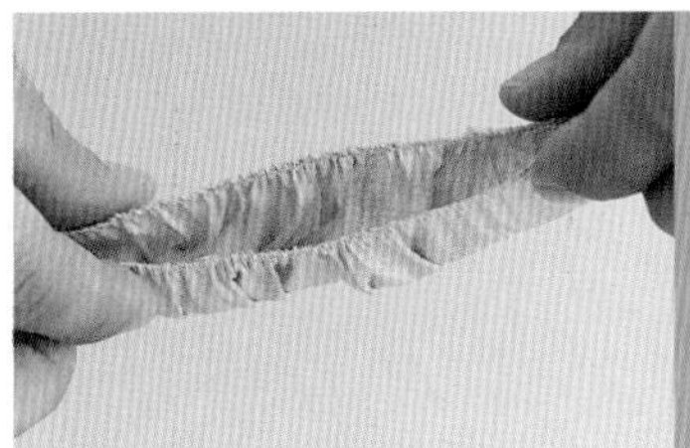

4) Fold the gathered ribbon in half lengthwise.

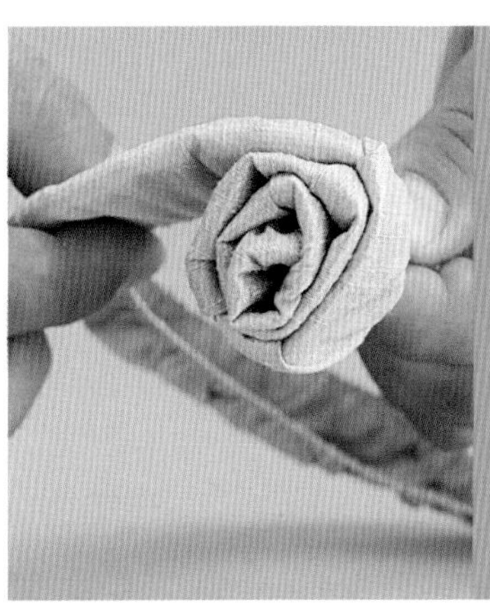

5) Beginning at the knot, roll the folded, gathered ribbon around the knot. This process will form the rose. When the rose is complete, secure the flower's shape by tying the excess wire around the knot at the base of the rose. Wrap florist's wire around that binding point to create a stem for the rose, and tape the wire stem with stem wrap.

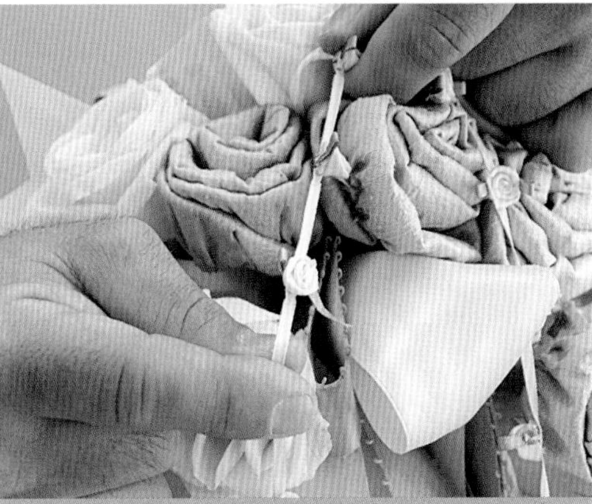

6) Gather the five six-loop bows together, and arrange the ribbon roses among the loops, to begin forming the bouquet. Wire and tape fresh roses, and arrange them into the bouquet at the last minute. Bind all the wire stems together with stem wrap, to create a handle by which to carry the bouquet. Add streamers of miniature rosette ribbon through the bouquet as a final touch.

tailored stems

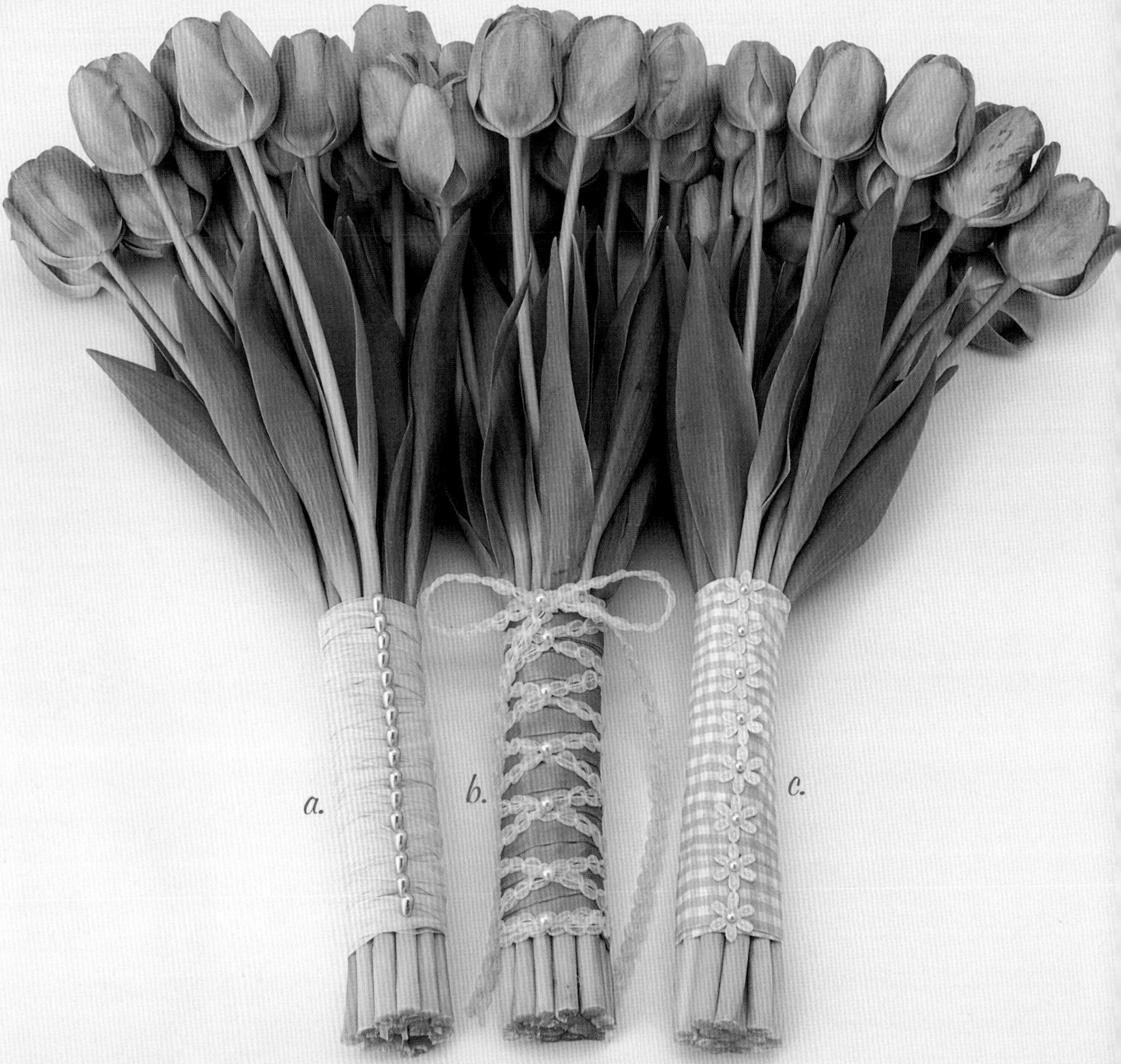

tailored stems

a. b. c.

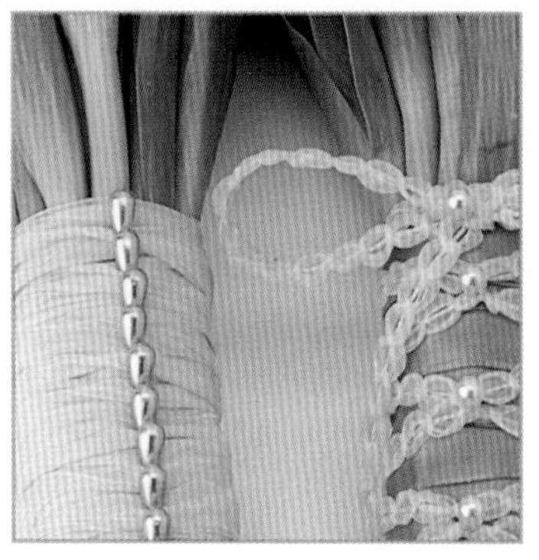

No ***bridesmaid's bouquet*** is complete without detailing the bare flower stems. These three options look intricate but are easy to complete. Beginning with a basic ribbon wrap around the stems of a hand-tied tulip bouquet, a variety of tailored accents can be added to create different looks. Novelty ribbons, available in everything from braids to die-cuts, add style with little effort.

a. how-to: precision pearls wrap

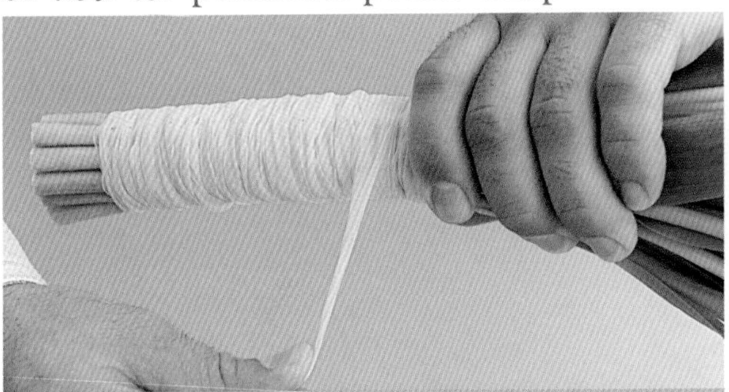

1) Wrap stems tightly with 1½-inch-wide ribbon, beginning just below the foliage. Scrunch the ribbon narrow as you wrap downward, for a full, dimensional look.

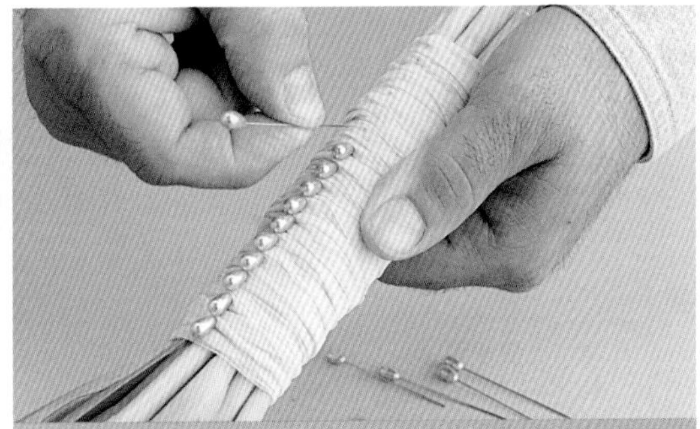

2) Decorate the ribbon wrap with colored pear-head corsage pins, inserting the pins at a downward angle, forming a straight line.

b. how-to: french-braid wrap

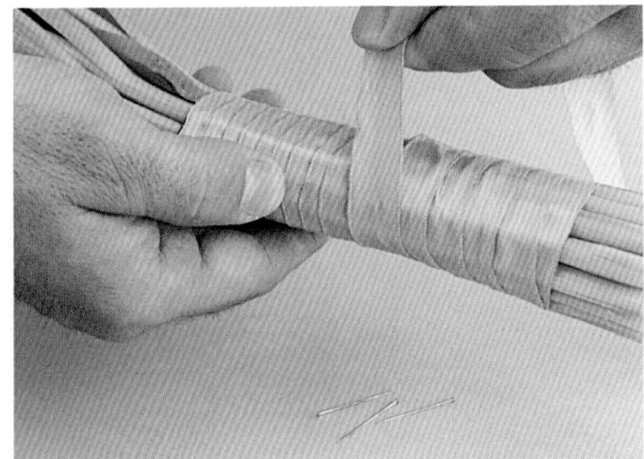

1) Beginning just below the foliage, wrap the stems with a ⅝-inch-wide ribbon. Wrap downward to near the bottom of the stems, then back to the top, keeping the ribbon flat and taut.
Note: Wrapping twice ensures a smooth and sturdy binding.

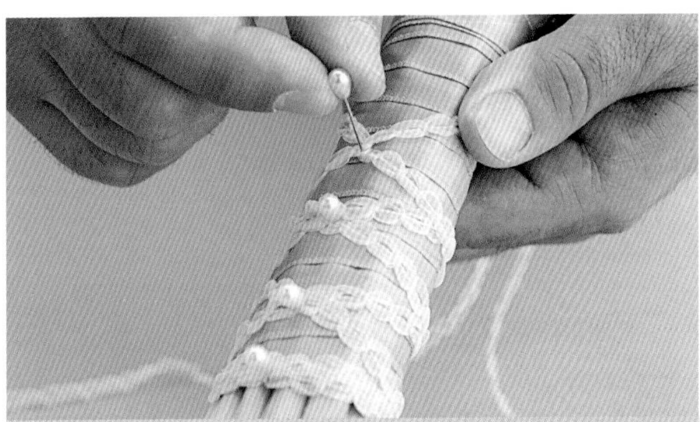

2) French-braid a contrasting ⅜-inch-wide decorative ribbon over the base ribbon. *(See the "French Braid" how-to on Page 17.)* Secure the ribbon at the twists with pear-head corsage pins.
Note: Cut pins short with a wire cutter so a straight insertion is possible without the pins protruding through the stems.

c. how-to: country casual wrap

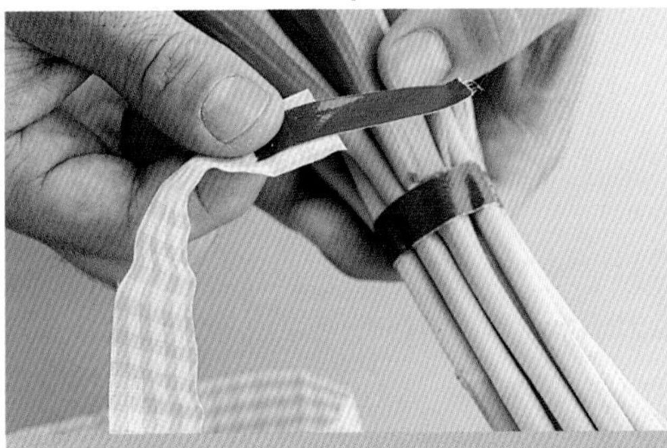

1) Secure ⅞-inch-wide checked ribbon to the bouquet binding with waterproof tape. Wrap the stems, working downward and then back to the top, keeping the ribbon taut and smooth. Secure the ribbon at the top with straight pins.

2) Tack a length of ⅝-inch-wide flower die-cut ribbon down the center of the ribbon wrap with small round-head corsage pins, placing a pin in the center of each ribbon flower.
Note: Cut the pins, if necessary, to keep the tips from protruding through the stems.

designer pillow

personal touches turn a ring-bearer's pillow into an artful accompaniment. Ribbons are woven across the pillow's face and secured at the edges with hot glue. The lace edging is painted brown to coordinate. An intricate ribbon braid adds a professional finish. The final touch is a cluster of spray roses and spray carnations tucked among ribbon loops and streamers.

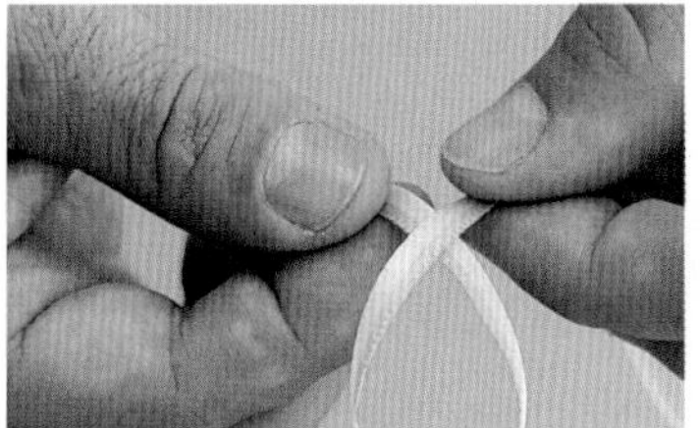

1) Make a loop in the center of a length of ¼-inch-wide single- or double-face satin ribbon by crossing the ribbon ends over each other.

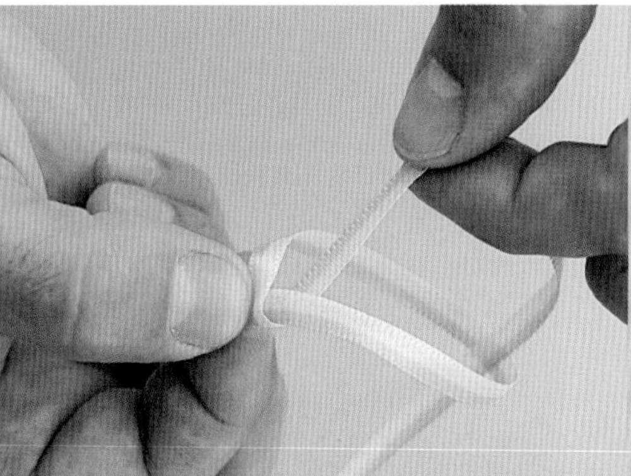

2) Fold the ribbon end that is on top behind, and pull it through the existing loop to create a new loop. If the ribbon is single-face, make sure the finished side faces up.

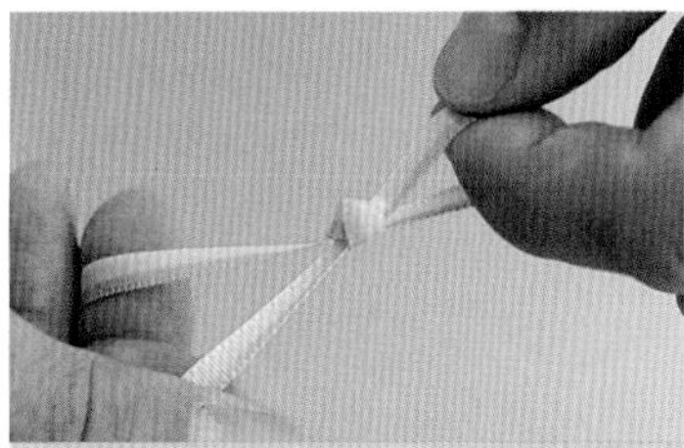

3) Pull the original loop taut to hold the new loop in place.
Note: This knot is referred to as a slipknot.

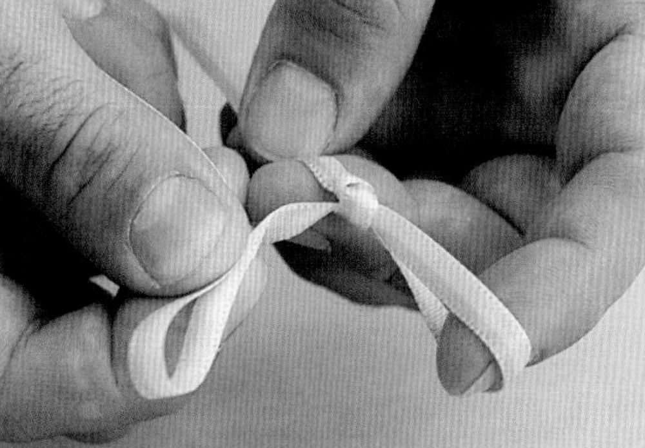

4) Create another loop with the opposite streamer (finished side of the ribbon up, if using single-face satin).

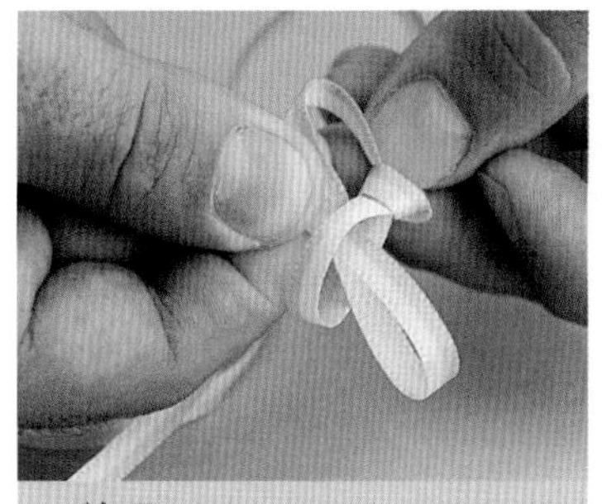

5) Thread the new loop through the previously formed loop.

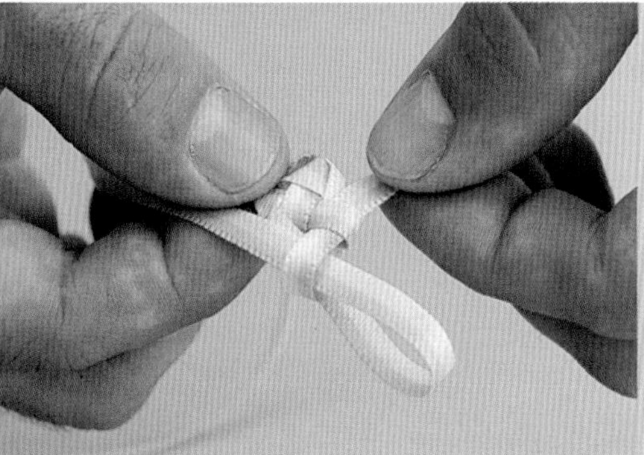

6) Pull the previous loop taut to hold the new loop. Pick up the opposite streamer and repeat Steps 4, 5 and 6. Continue braiding until the desired length is reached.
Note: You will need a length of ribbon approximately four times the length of the desired finished braid.

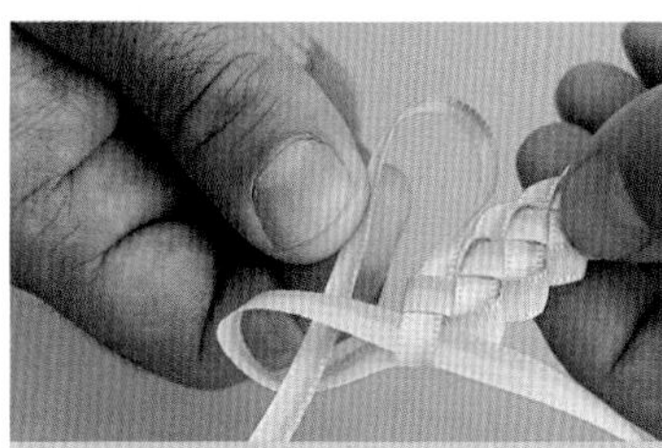

7) When you have created the braid to the desired length, pull the last loop all the way through, and tighten. This will leave two flat ribbon streamers, and the braid will hold secure.

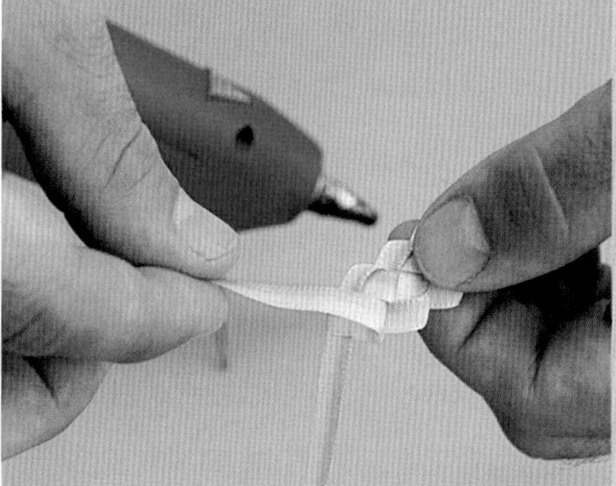

8) Carefully fold the two ribbon ends, one after the other, over the end and to the back of the braid. Secure them in place with hot glue. Trim the excess ribbon for a neat finish. Secure the braid around the pillow's perimeter with hot glue.

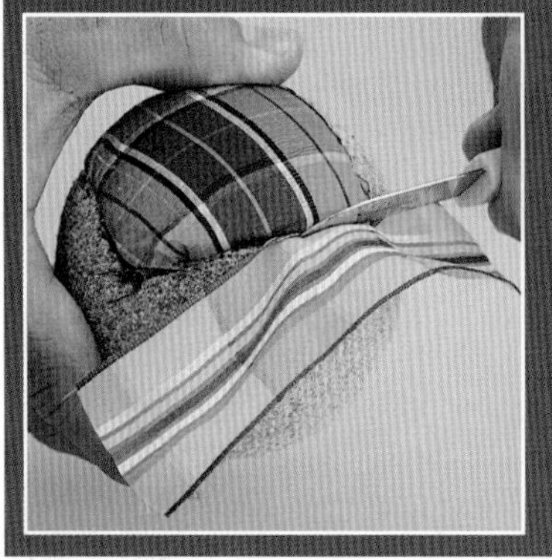

crisp autumn days invite a bounteous crop of colors, textures and patterns. Harvest your creativity with a cornucopia of design ideas for wreaths, centerpieces and other riches of the season.

(harvest)

stylish *weave*

Satin ribbons *woven* through the stems of a fan-shaped composition of callas serve not only a decorative purpose but also a structural one. The tension maintains the fan shape while allowing full use of the elegant, elongated stems. And the sleek weave is stylish but less fussy than a bow, making this a suitable gift for a man or to display in an office or other formal setting.

how-to: woven stems

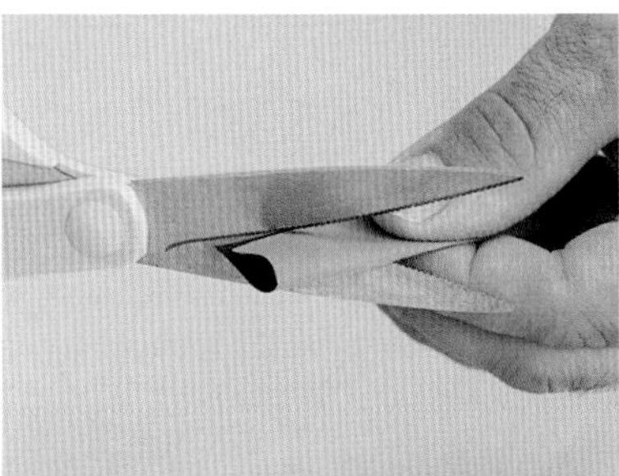

1) Trim the ends of lengths of 1½-inch-wide wire-edge double-face satin ribbon with inverted "V"-patterned cuts (a.k.a. dovetail or chevron cuts) by folding the edges of each end of ribbon together lengthwise and making a diagonal cut upward from the edges to the center fold.

2) Beginning at the base of the arrangement, knot one end of a length of ribbon around a calla stem on one edge of the arrangement, and weave the ribbon horizontally through the stems, to the opposite edge of the arrangement.

3) Continue weaving lengths of ribbon, in rows, through the calla stems, alternating front and back from the row below.

4) Knot the opposite ends of the lengths of ribbon around the calla stems on the other edge of the arrangement.

denim décor

wreath and wall pocket combine in this clever and casual door or wall adornment. Denim ribbon is a neutral backdrop to match any flower or color scheme, and the pocket from an old pair of jeans creates a receptacle for the permanent blooms. Because the flowers are simply dropped in, they are easy to change out seasonally, so this wreath can be displayed year-round.

how-to: denim-covered wreath

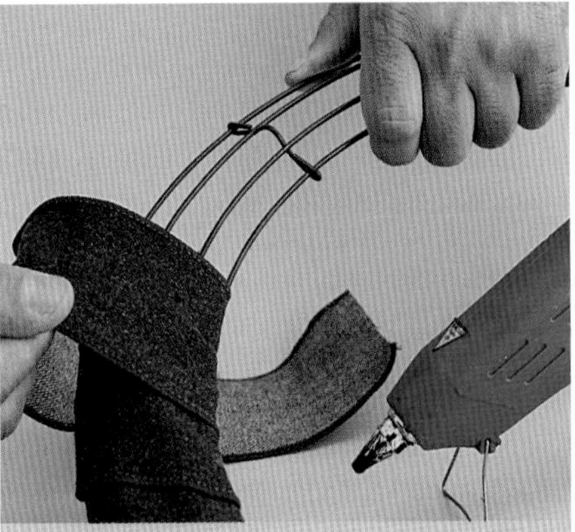

1) Wrap a wire wreath form with 2⅜-inch-wide wire-edge denim ribbon, keeping the ribbon taut and overlapping it to cover the form.

2) Wrap a length of the denim ribbon, with its ends cut into inverted "V"s (a.k.a. dovetail or chevron cuts), around the wreath form, to create a hanger, and wire the ends together with a two-loop bow, the tails of which are also cut into inverted "V"s.

3) Glue a denim pocket, cut from an old pair of jeans, to the bottom of the wreath.

4) Cut a piece of foam-centered board or heavy cardboard to fit inside the pocket. This will keep the pocket sturdy and taut. Arrange permanent flowers into the pocket.

Note: The flowers can be kept in place by dipping the stems into hot-melt (pan) glue before arranging them into the pocket.

buckets of personality

buckets of personality

A solid-colored French *flower bucket* becomes a one-of-a-kind vessel with a pretty patchwork and button treatment. The ribbon hues complement the florals—lilies, roses, bells-of-Ireland, *Hypericum* and wild oats—and leaf-shaped buttons are a fun addition. This is a great way to showcase larger ribbon patterns and tailor a container to the flowers used or the recipient's interests.

how-to: patchwork container

1) Cut pieces of various patterns of ribbon into an assortment of sizes and shapes with pinking shears.

2) Glue the patches, in a random pattern, onto the container with spray adhesive. Adhere decorative buttons to the container with hot glue.

how-to: ribbon loops

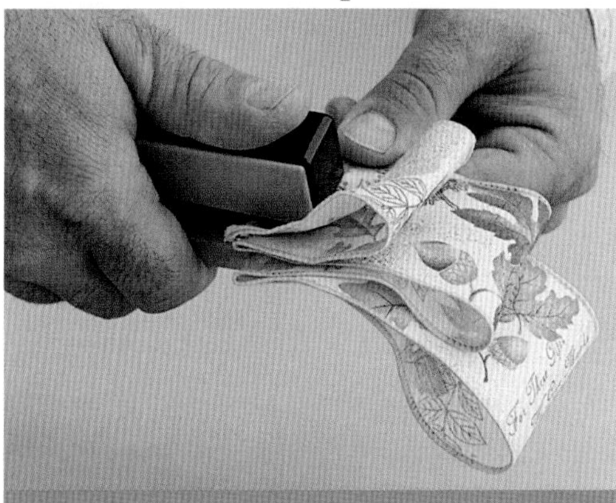

1) Form a three-loop "half Dior bow" from a length of 2⅜-inch-wide patterned or print ribbon. The loops should be graduated in size, from small to large. Staple the ends to hold the loops in place.

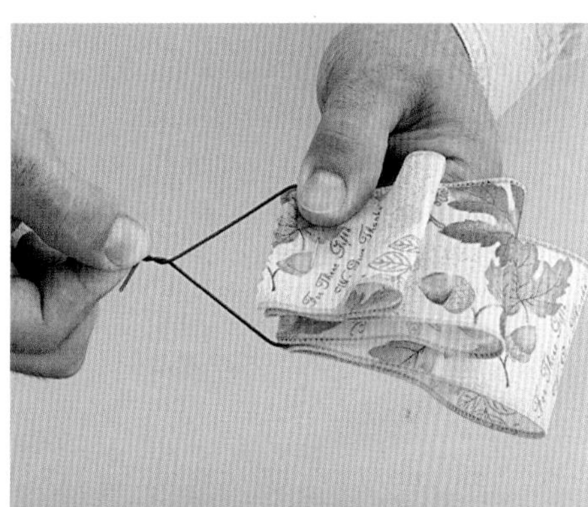

2) Thread a piece of heavy-gauge enameled florist's wire through the stapled end of the loops. Twist the ends of the wire together, and insert the wire into the arrangement.

earthy elements

Metallics *sparkle* and textures *tempt* in this eclectic setting for a dinner party or event. Roses, *Leucospermums* and *Hypericum* fill a river-cane-covered container adorned with a handcrafted medallion. The centerpiece could serve on its own as a masculine gift. Shimmering ribbons coordinate the votive candleholders and napkin rings, and mesh fabric serves as a place mat.

how-to: medallion

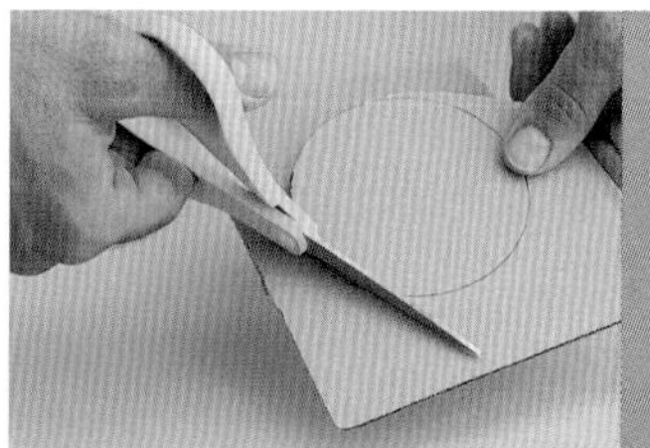

1) Cut a circle from a piece of cardboard.

2) Glue pieces of 1½-inch-wide sheer metallic patterned ribbon and ⅝-inch-wide open-weave metallic ribbon to the cardboard with spray adhesive. Overlap and change directions with the coordinating ribbons to cover the circle. Add feathers and jewels with spray adhesive.

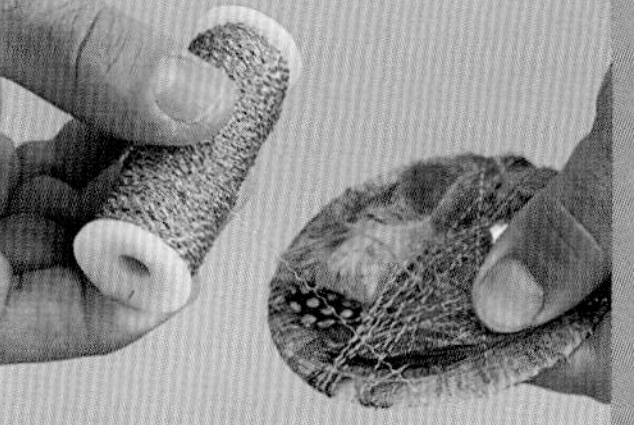

3) Wrap the medallion with bullion wire, crisscrossing to create an interesting pattern and hold the glued items securely.

4) Twist together several ribbons of varying patterns and texture with metallic tinsel cording to create a rope-like effect. Wrap the "rope" horizontally around the midsection of the river-cane-covered container. Glue the medallion in the front and center of the container with hot glue.

how-to: napkin ring

1) Knot two lengths of 1½-inch-wide ribbon (either the same or coordinating patterns) together in two places, on both sides of the center of the ribbons. Leave a space between the knots large enough to slip a napkin through the two pieces of ribbon.

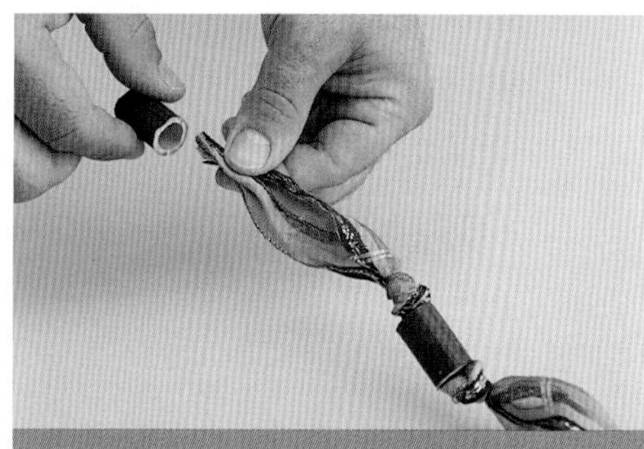

2) Thread beads and short pieces of river cane onto the ribbons, knotting the ribbons before and after each addition. Cut inverted "V" patterns (a.k.a. dovetail or chevron cuts) into the ribbon ends.

tulip *twirls*

tulip *twirls*

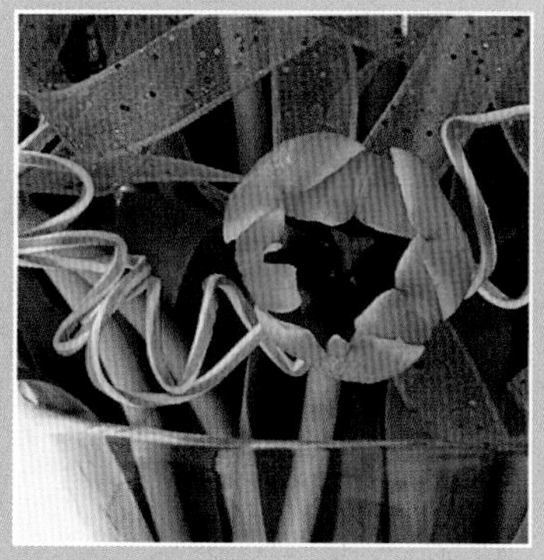

Sparkling *whorled ribbons and curlicues* highlight a festive arrangement for a party or a celebratory bouquet. The springy coils convey spontaneity and excitement while mirroring the implied motion of the swirled tulips in the base of the design. Any monobotanical composition can be enhanced with this technique, which allows for fewer flowers while still achieving a lush look.

how-to: curly ribboned stems

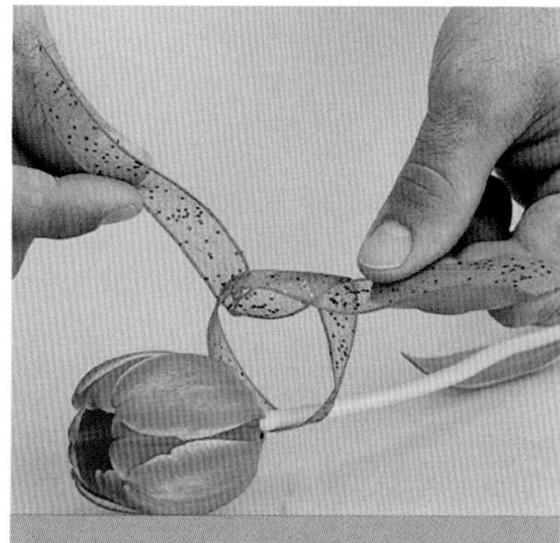

1) Tie a length of ⅝-inch-wide wire-edge ribbon in a single knot on each flower stem, just below the flower head.

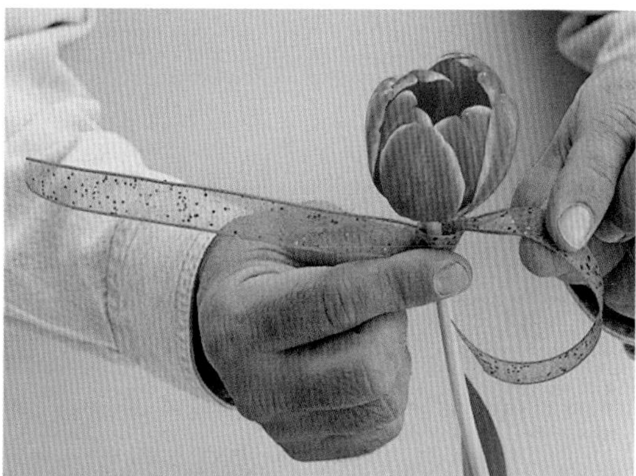

2) Curl each length of ribbon by pressing it between your thumb and forefinger and sliding them down the ribbon. Arrange the flowers into the vase.

how-to: curlicues

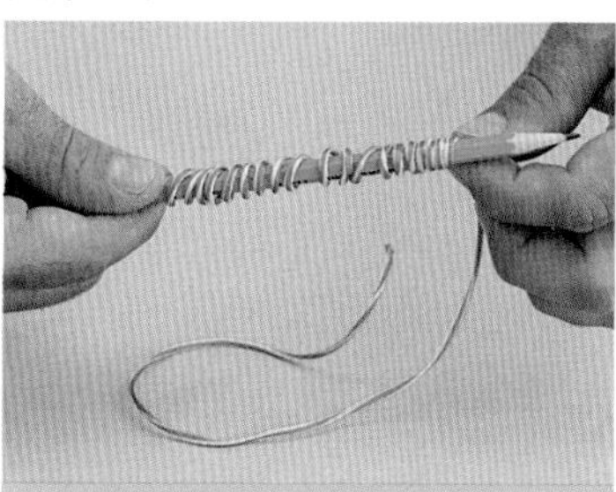

1) Wrap a length of narrow wired satin cording around a pencil, and slide it off, creating a curlicue. Make several of these.

2) Tuck the curlicues among the flowers.

bedecked *baskets*

bedecked baskets

Unadorned plant baskets gain *style and personality* with the addition of ruffly ribbon treatments. A mix of purple patterns and tan complements the blond baskets and their colorful contents—a *Phalaenopsis* orchid plant and an African violet plant—but the ribbon choices can reflect any décor. The ribbon accessories can be changed out easily to correspond with each new season.

how-to: ruffled collar

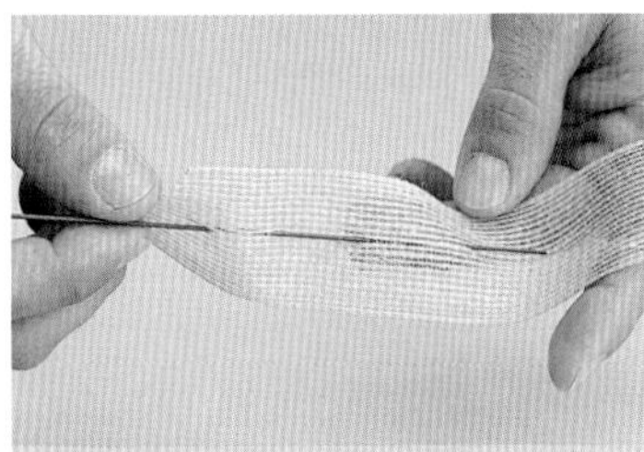

1) "Stitch" through the center of a length of 1½-inch-wide unwired open-weave ribbon with a piece of florist's wire.

2) Bend the wire back at one end, creating a hook, to hold it in place. Gather the ribbon along the wire to create a ruffle. Encircle the basket rim with the ruffle, securing it to the basket with hot glue. Next, tie two coordinating purple ribbons of varying widths (⅝-inch and 1⅜-inch widths are shown on opposite page) to the handle, catching the orchid stem to hold the bloom spike in place.

how-to: basket edge and handle treatments

1) Make several two-loop bows, with tails, of coordinating patterns of ribbon (⅝-inch, 1½-inch and 2⅜-inch widths, in plaid, gingham, grosgrain and satin-edge sheer, are shown here). Attach the bows to the basket rim with hot glue, placing them closely together to cover the edge.

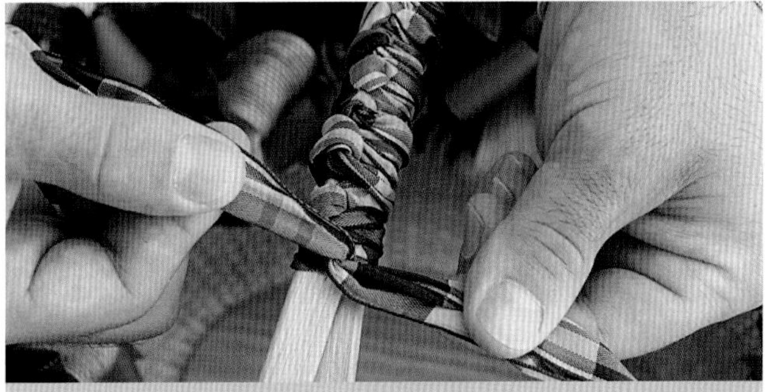

2) French-braid ribbon onto the basket handle: Center a length of ribbon underneath the handle. Bring both ends of the ribbon from beneath the handle upward, over the top of the handle. Overlap the two ends of the ribbon, and twist each end 180 degrees, returning each ribbon in the direction from which it came. Cross the ribbon ends underneath the handle, and repeat the process until the desired amount of handle is covered. Knot the ends of the ribbon underneath the handle, and secure the knot in place with hot glue.

faux fruit

a pumpkin crafted of open-weave ribbon, topped with a branch stem and permanent leaf, is the focal point in this seasonal design of dried delights, but the fabric fruit easily could stand on its own. Satin-edge sheer ribbon on the basket handle, tacked into loose loops with paper-covered wire, complements the hues of the *Hydrangeas*, wheat, yarrow, thistles, clovers and berries.

how-to: ribbon pumpkin

1) Cut indentations into opposite ends of a plastic-foam ball to create the top and bottom of the pumpkin.

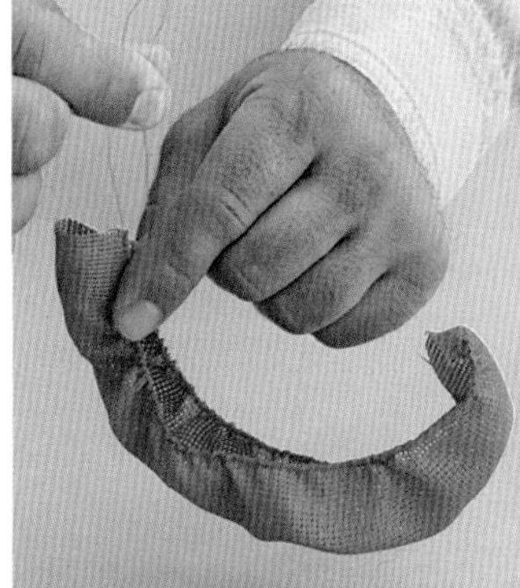

2) Fold a length of 2½-inch-wide wire-edge open-weave ribbon in half lengthwise, and crimp one end to hold the wires secure. Beginning at the opposite end, pull both wires simultaneously, gathering the ribbon along the wires. Repeat this process until you have enough sections to cover the ball.

3) Attach one end of a gathered ribbon section to the plastic-foam ball at the indentation with a hairpin-shaped wire.

4) Turn the ball over and attach the other end of the ribbon near the opposite indentation. Continue attaching gathered ribbon sections until the ball is covered. Shape the ribbon as you go, keeping it firm but avoiding pulling it too tight. The indentations make it possible to tuck the ribbon ends into the ball to help create the pumpkin shape.

knotted wraps

luxury and fun combine in a technique that customizes a plain glass vase—in this case, a narrow rectangle. Mixing velvet, satin and sheer ribbons adds texture, and selecting a range of browns and golds evokes classic elegance. The walnuts are a nod to the season. Try this on other shapes of vases and with other accents, such as berries, candies or cherries, as well as with other color themes.

how-to: ribbon stripe vase

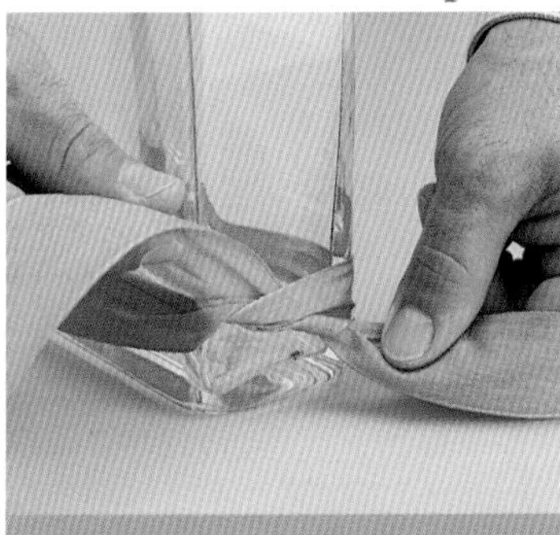

1) Tie a length of 1½-inch-wide unwired ribbon around the bottom of the vase, and knot.

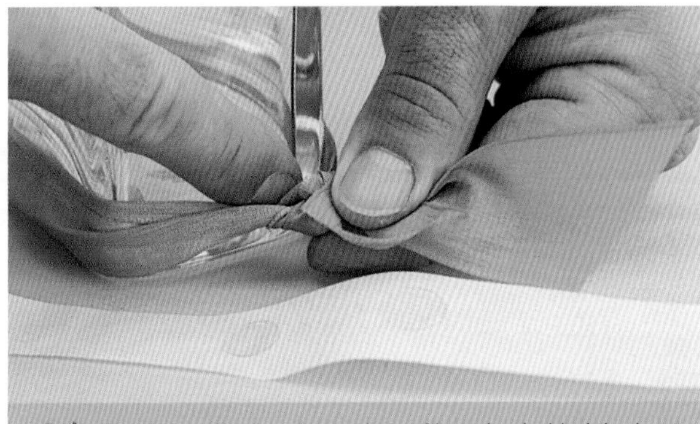

2) Place an adhesive dot or drop of hot glue behind the knot to secure the ribbon in place on the vase.

3) Continue tying various types of unwired ribbons, in coordinating patterns and/or colors and varying widths (⅝-inch, ⅞-inch and 1½-inch widths are shown here) onto the vase. Position the ribbons close together, overlapping them slightly, and adhere each knot to the vase with an adhesive dot or hot glue. Trim all the ribbon ends with diagonal cuts.

4) Hot-glue fresh or permanent walnuts randomly between the ribbon knots.

patchwork spheres

patchwork spheres

A bowl of *textured orbs* is a popular home accent, and this trendy update adapts to any decorating scheme with different choices of ribbons. A crazy-quilt effect is created here with various plaid ribbons in differing widths. Monobotanical spheres of fresh carnations, billy buttons and spray chrysanthemums round out the collection.

how-to: ribbon-covered orbs

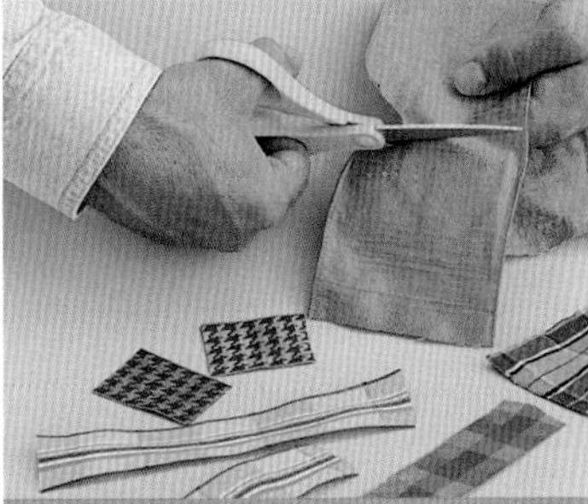

1) Cut pieces of wire-edge ribbons, in coordinating patterns, into squares, rectangles and triangles. A combination of 1½-inch-wide, 2¼-inch-wide and 3½-inch-wide ribbons are used in these examples.

2) Using a knife, press the edges of a square piece of ribbon into a plastic-foam ball. Continue around the square's edges until the ribbon is completely embedded into the ball. *Note: A 4-inch-diameter ball is shown in this example, but any size ball can be used.*

3) Place a rectangular piece of ribbon adjacent to the square piece, and press one edge into one of the square piece's indentations. Continue pressing around the rectangle with the knife, making new indentations, until it is completely embedded into the plastic foam.

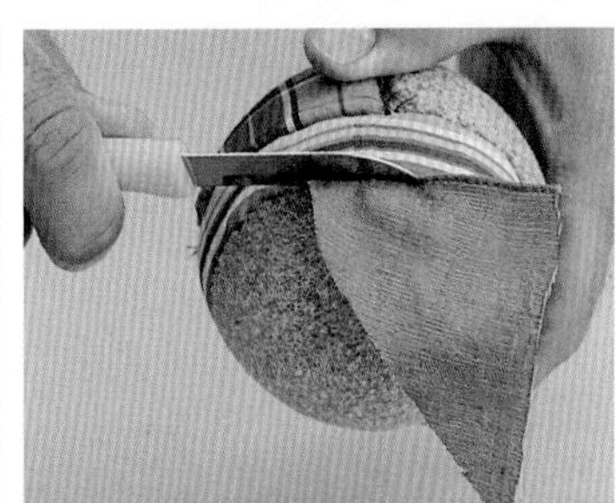

4) Press a triangular piece of ribbon alongside the rectangular piece until it, too, is embedded into the plastic foam. Continue alternating ribbon pieces until the ball is covered.

it's the most wonderful time of the year, and holiday revelry inspires festive decorations, from traditional trappings to those with contemporary appeal. Ribbons make wreaths, packages and all holiday projects sing.

(Christmas)

tasseled tower

To *dazzle* gift recipients, try a contemporary stacked presentation of multiple packages and a fresh flower arrangement. A shimmering ribbon tassel takes the place of a bow and adds an elegant accent. The same multicolored cording that binds and suspends the tassel is used to secure the hand-tied bouquet of tulips and pine, uniting the presentation.

how-to: ribbon tassel

1) Cut several equal-length pieces of 1½-inch-wide metallic-striped sheer ribbon, and cut inverted "V" patterns (a.k.a. dovetail or chevron cuts) into the ends. Fold one end of each piece of ribbon in half lengthwise, and pin that end to a small plastic-foam ball. Continue layering ribbons atop each other until a full tassel is created.

2) Tightly secure the ribbons below the ball with florist's wire. Trim the excess wire.

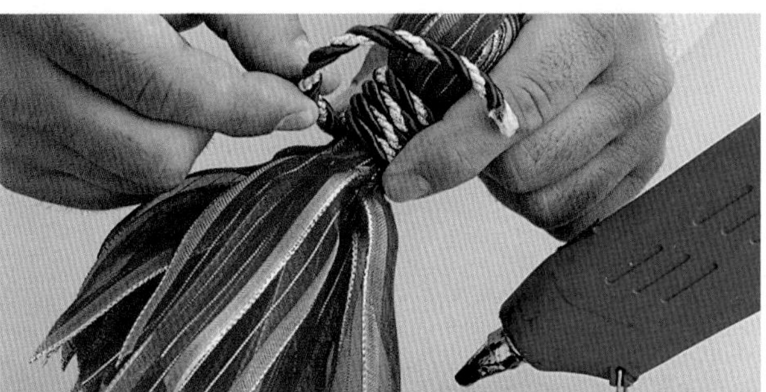

3) Wrap cording multiple times around the point where the ribbon is bound with wire, and below, forming a coiled band. Glue the ends in place with hot glue.

Note: Wrap the ends of the cording with clear tape to prevent unraveling.

4) Make a loop from the cording, and attach it to the top of the ribbon-covered plastic-foam ball with a cluster of colored corsage pins. In addition to securing the loop to the tassel, the pins provide a decorative accent.

gifts with a *twist*

a. b. c. d.

Clear glass vases are *transformed* into custom gifts with a quartet of tying techniques, from fluffed and flirty to trim and tailored. Monobotanical arrangements, with evergreen accents, are ideal for these highly decorative yuletide containers. These techniques also are adaptable for any season or theme.

a. how-to: pinwheel bow

Tie a length of 1½-inch-wide ribbon around the neck of a vase. Cut a collection of 1½-inch-wide ribbons into equal lengths, trimming the ends with inverted "V"-patterned cuts (a.k.a. dovetail or chevron cuts). Gather the ribbons into a group, crimp them in the center and tie them onto the vase with the ribbon around the neck of the vase. Glue a jewel into the center with hot glue.

b. how-to: necktie

Tie a length of 2½-inch-wide ribbon around the neck of a vase to form a "necktie." Cut the ends into a necktie-style point by folding the edges of the ribbon together lengthwise and making a diagonal cut downward from the edges to the center fold.

c. how-to: rows of bows

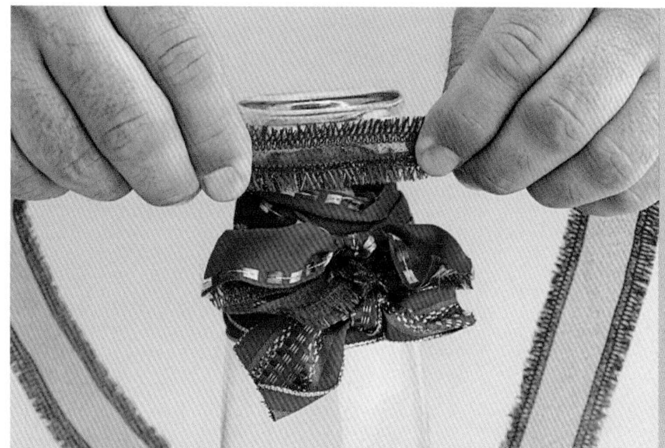

Tie lengths of ribbons, in various widths and patterns, around a vase, one atop another, beginning near the midsection of the vase and working upward to the neck or rim. This technique involves securing the center of a length of ribbon in the "front" of the vase with an adhesive dot or hot glue, then wrapping the ends around to the opposite side ("backside") of the vase and back around to the front, tying them in a knot, and trimming them with diagonal cuts. Repeat this procedure with coordinating ribbons, "stacking" the ribbons, until the neck of the vase is reached.

d. how-to: french braid

Create a widely spaced French braid from 1½-inch-wide ribbon: Secure the center of a length of ribbon with an adhesive dot to the "backside" of a tapered vase, at the base. Bring the ends of the ribbon around to the opposite ("front") side of the vase at a slightly upward angle; overlap and twist them; and return each end, in the direction it came from, horizontally, to the back of the vase. Cross and twist the ends in the back, and return them to the front, working up the vase. Repeat this procedure until you reach the neck or rim of the vase, then tie the ribbon into a dramatic bow, with streamers, on the backside of the vase. Hot-glue jewels to the twists on the front side of the vase.

forever-green *wreath*

*kid-friendly project

A *festive,* versatile wreath takes full advantage of the many fashionable patterns and fabrics that are available in ribbon today, and simple knots make it easy to assemble. By keeping all of the knots at the outer edge of the wreath form and letting the tails extend outward, a three-dimensional effect is achieved. Coordinating ribbons wrap cylinder vases to complete an entryway or mantel display.

how-to: ribbon-wrapped wreath

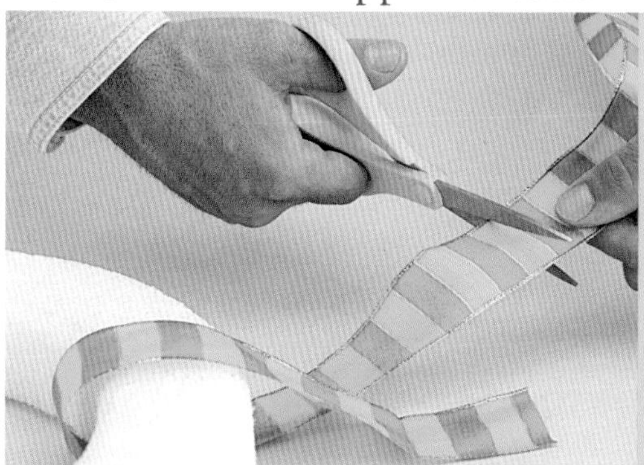

1) Determine the length the pieces of ribbon need to be for this project by wrapping one ribbon around the plastic foam and cutting it to the desired length. Use this piece of ribbon as a pattern, and cut additional pieces of ribbon, in coordinating patterns and widths, enough to cover the wreath form.

Note: Nine different sheer metallic ribbons, in various widths from ⅞ inch to 4 inches and patterns including solids, plaids, stripes and polka dots, were used in this wreath.

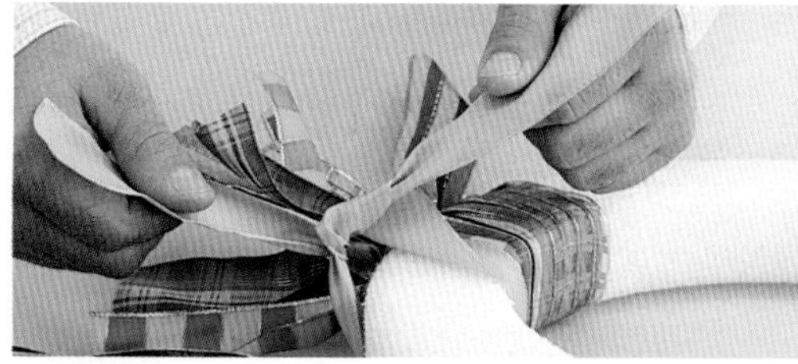

2) Tie the ribbons, one at a time, around the wreath form, knotting each on the outer edge of the form. Slightly overlap each successive ribbon so the wreath form is fully covered.

3) Trim the ribbon ends with inverted "V"-patterned cuts (a.k.a. dovetail or chevron cuts) by folding the edges of each end together lengthwise and making a diagonal cut upward from the edges to the center fold to complete the wreath.

how-to: ribbon-wrapped vase

For the coordinating vases, wrap coordinating ribbons around glass cylinder vases, securing the ribbons in place with spray adhesive *(see the technique used in "Custom Candlescape" on Page 29)*.

party plaids

Luxurious *silk and velvet* ribbons combine to unite varied containers and the place setting for a festive holiday meal. The banding technique used on the napkin also adds style to the vases filled with tulips, roses, *Viburnums*, *Hypericum* and evergreens. And the woven mat can be re-created in any size, as a table runner or to anchor a centerpiece.

how-to: place mat

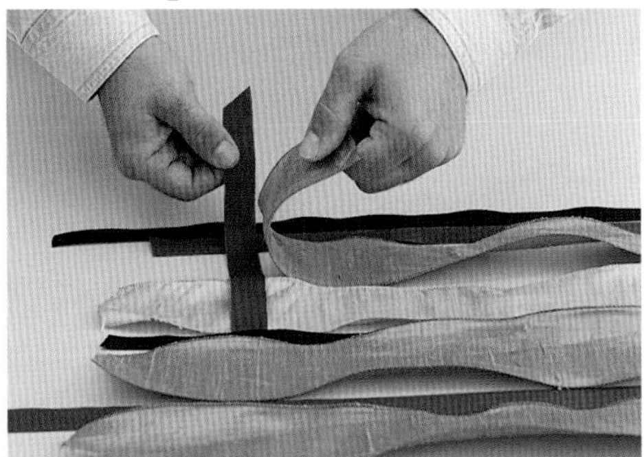

1) Lay lengths of ribbon in horizontal strips as the first step in weaving the plaid place mat. Use a combination of ribbons (5/8-inch, 7/8-inch and 2½-inch widths in moss, chartreuse, red and black are shown here, but any widths and colors can be used). Tape the ends of the horizontal ribbons to the table to hold them in place. Then, beginning in the center, weave other strips of ribbon vertically, one at a time, in an over-and-under manner, through the horizontal strips, securing them with hot glue where needed. Alternate colors and widths to create an interesting pattern.

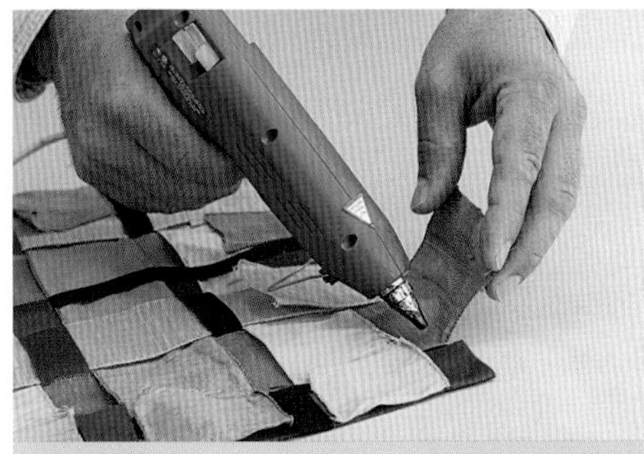

2) When complete, flip the place mat over, fold the ribbon ends back and secure them with hot glue. The place mat can be backed with a piece of coordinating fabric or felt, if desired.

how-to: candle wrap

Secure one end of a length of a plaid ribbon to one side of a square glass votive candleholder with hot glue. Wrap the ribbon around the glass, and secure the other end over the first with hot glue. Wrap coordinating velvet cording around the votive holder, just below the top, and tie it into a two-loop "shoestring" bow. Knot the ends of the cording.

Note: A 4-inch-wide ribbon covers this entire votive candleholder, but a narrower width could be used if you wish to leave some of the glass exposed.

how-to: napkin ring

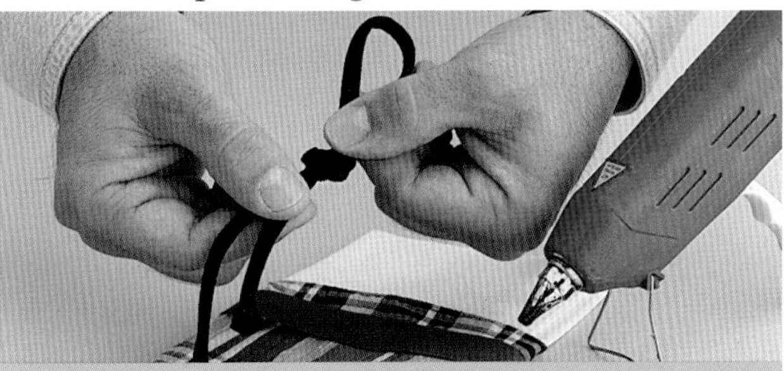

Wrap another length of the ribbon used to cover the votive candle-holder around the midsection of a napkin, and hot-glue one end over the other on the "backside" of the napkin. Wrap a coordinating ribbon, in a narrower width, over the first, and hot-glue its ends together. Create a knotted loop with the cording, knot the ends of the tails, and hot-glue it onto the ribbon band. Hot-glue fresh ever-greens and berries on as a fresh floral accent.

contemporary candle ring

Floral *candle rings* are traditional holiday accessories, but this modern update adds a new twist, being "suspended" around the center of a hurricane vase. Permanent *Hydrangeas* and blackberries and preserved reindeer moss are glued among the loops of green, gold and brown ribbons, which mirror the container's striped hues.

how-to: "suspended" candle ring

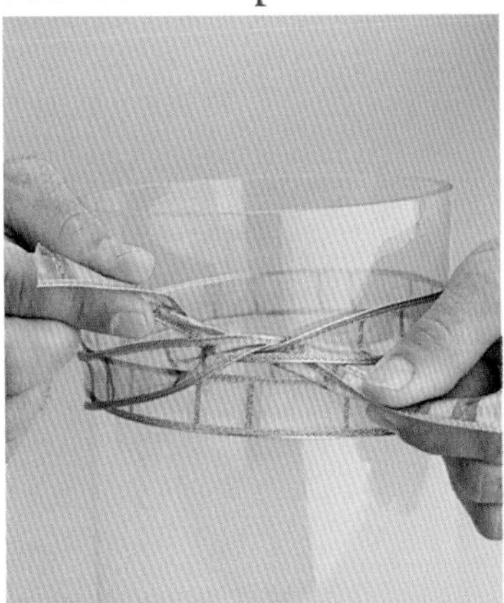

1) Wrap a length of ⅞-inch-wide ribbon around a hurricane glass twice, and tie the ends tightly in a knot.

2) Loosely thread coordinating patterns of ⅝-inch-wide and ⅞-inch-wide wire-edge and unwired ribbons through the ribbon that is tied to the vase, creating an artful but tangled mass of ribbons into which you can glue floral materials. *(The wire-edge ribbons create support for the florals, and the unwired ribbons add a softer look.)* Continue adding ribbons until the desired fullness is achieved. Shape the wire-edge ribbons to achieve maximum depth, rhythm and interest.

3) Adhere permanent flowers, berries and moss among the ribbons with hot-melt (pan) glue.

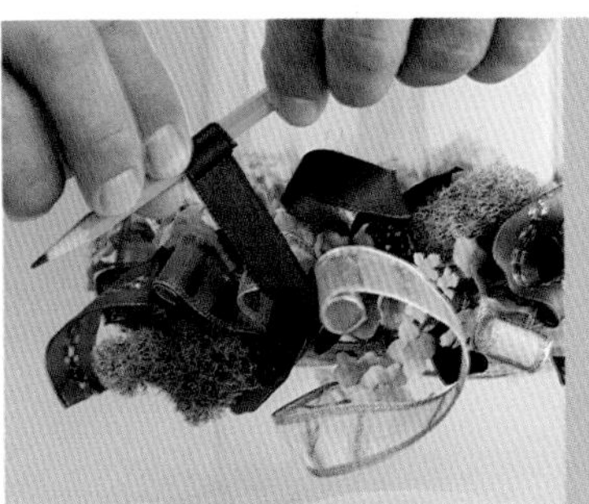

4) Wrap the wire-edge ribbon tails around a pencil to curl them.

seasonal *mosaic*

*kid-friendly project

The *interplay of hues* in a single color family creates depth and interest in this wreath and vase. Velvet ribbons offer a sumptuous but muted look that complements the textures of the roses and carnations, which are displayed in the same tone-on-tone hues. Colored-head corsage pins ensure speedy application of the wreath's ribbon squares and add a touch of pearly glamour.

how-to: ribbon "tile" wreath

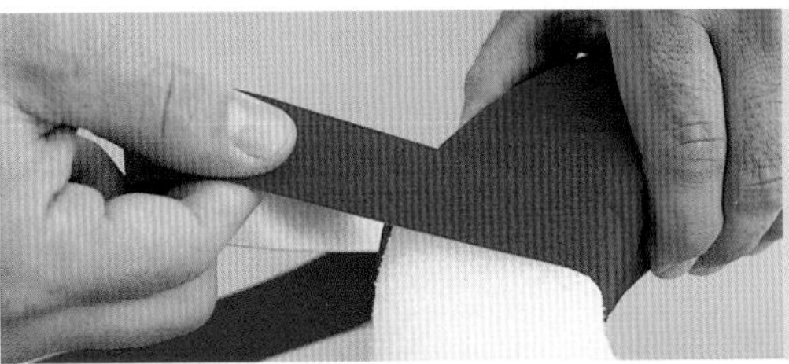

1) Wrap a plastic-foam wreath form with 2½-inch-wide velvet ribbon, keeping the ribbon taut and flat. After covering the form, secure the ribbon end to the backside with straight pins.

2) Cut squares from 2½-inch-wide velvet ribbon in at least three tints, tones or shades of your chosen hue.

3) Pin the ribbon squares onto the wreath form in random fashion with colored-head corsage pins in a coordinating hue to finish the wreath.

how-to: ribbon "tile" vase

Glue additional squares of ribbon onto a colored vase with spray adhesive. Overlap the squares in a random pattern.

couture accent

A fabric flower, fashioned from *plaid* silk ribbon, accents a stately pillar candle centered in a bed of incense cedar and pine cones. The same plaid ribbon also is folded into a band and laid atop a sheer black ribbon with stitched edges, both of which are glued to the edges of a metallic container.

how-to: ribbon flower

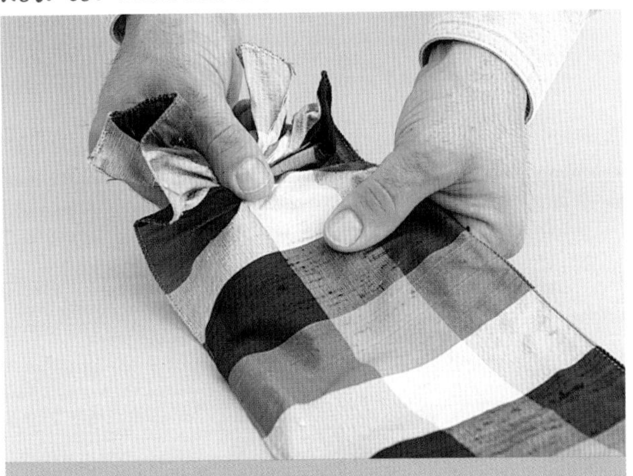

1) Gather a length of 6-inch-wide wire-edge ribbon, scrunching it through the center lengthwise.

2) Tightly bind the center of the gathered ribbon with florist's wire. Fluff out the ribbon edges to form a flowerlike creation.

3) Insert colored-head corsage pins, in a cluster, into the center of the flower.

4) Tape the ends of the wire and pins with stem wrap, then tape this "stem" to a wood pick with stem wrap, and insert the fabric flower into the design.

christmas *confections*

Reminiscent of ubiquitous ***peppermint*** Christmas candies, these red-and-white creations are equally delectable. Patterned and detailed ribbons add fanciful flair to the solid-colored spheres of fresh carnations. The varying heights and placements of the ribbons give depth to the grouping, which would look stunning as a centerpiece.

a. how-to: ribbon-loop base

Create a six-loop bow, with streamers, from 1½-inch-wide wire-edge patterned sheer ribbon. Add two extra lengths of ribbon to the bow to create four additional streamers. Flatten the bow on top of a glass candlestick, and place a carnation sphere on top. Cut inverted "V" patterns (a.k.a. dovetail or chevron cuts) into the ribbon ends.

b. how-to: bunched ribbon encirclement

Fold over one end of a length of 2½-inch-wide wire-edge sheer ribbon to hold the wires in place. At the opposite end, pull both wires simultaneously, gathering the ribbon along the wires. Fold over the wire ends to hold the gathered ribbon in place. Wrap the gathered ribbon around a carnation sphere, and wire the ends together at the top of the sphere. Insert a four-loop bow, with tails, secured to a wired wood pick, through the intersection of the ribbon ends to secure the gathered ribbon and adorn the sphere. *Note: Tape the wood pick with stem wrap, or leave a small section of wire between the bow and the pick, to prevent the wood pick from wicking water from the floral-foam sphere and wetting the ribbon.*

c. how-to: curled ribbon encirclement

Wrap a length of 1½-inch-wide decorative ribbon around a carnation sphere, and tie the ends of the ribbon into a two-loop bow, leaving extra-long streamers. Wrap the streamers tightly around a pencil to curl them.

d. how-to: ribbon-bow base

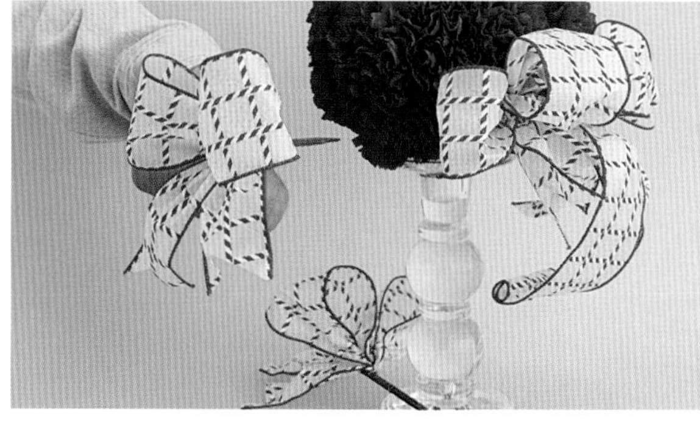

Make several two-loop bows, with streamers, from 2½-inch-wide patterned ribbon, and attach them to wired wood picks. Place a carnation sphere atop a glass candlestick. Surround the base of the sphere with the bows, inserting the wood picks directly into the floral-foam-centered sphere. Cut inverted "V" patterns (a.k.a. dovetail or chevron cuts) into the ribbon ends, or wrap the ends around a pencil, to finish.

festive *forest*

sleek ribbon trees are just the right size for decorating small spaces, such as tabletops, mantels and even desktops. Inexpensive gold tussie-mussies cap the trees, which rest on upside-down mint-julep cups. Vary the sizes of the cone forms and bases to create an interesting group, and experiment with other embellishments to personalize these tiny tannenbaums.

how-to: ribbon trees

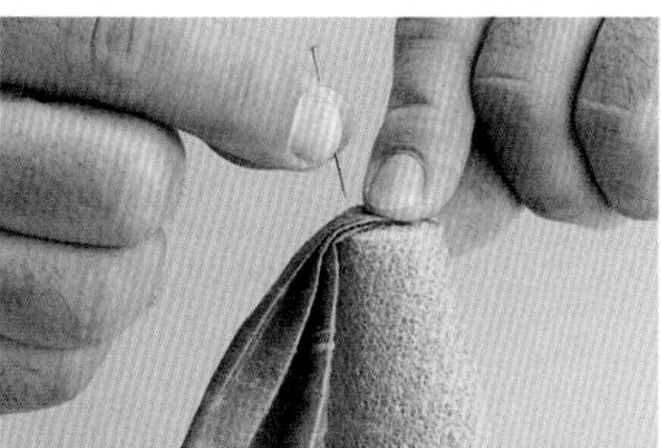

1) Gather one end of a length of ribbon, and attach it, with a straight pin, to the top of a plastic-foam cone. Spread out the ribbon going toward the bottom of the cone.

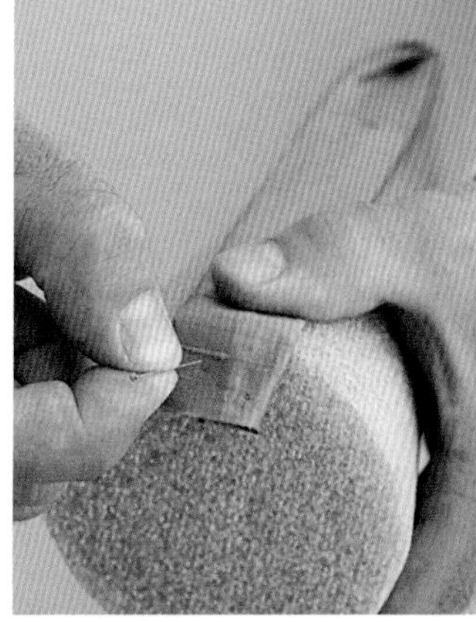

2) Fold the opposite end of the ribbon under the cone, and secure it to the base with straight pins. Repeat these two steps until the conical form is covered.

Note: A combination of $1\frac{1}{2}$-inch-wide and $2\frac{1}{2}$-inch-wide wire-edge ribbons is shown here, with a focus on texture, incorporating velvets, sheers and metallic accents.

3) Cluster groups of colored round-head corsage pins to create an ornament effect.

4) Pin cording at the top of the "tree," and wrap the cording around the tree to the bottom, creating a garland effect. Fold the cording under the tree, and secure it in place with straight pins.

Note: Wrap the ends of the cording with clear tape to prevent unraveling.

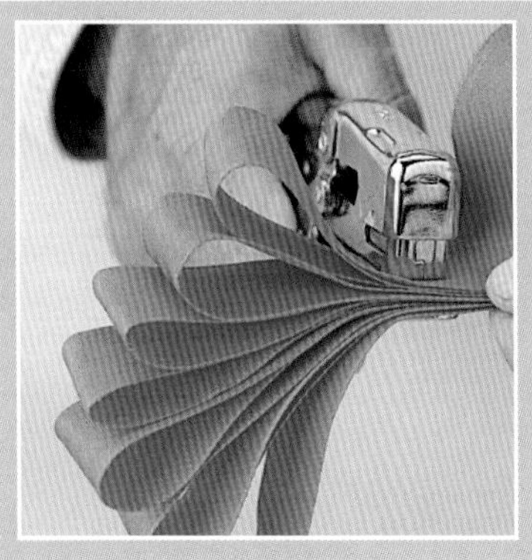

step-by-step instructions for creating five popular bows, each of which has a variety of decorative applications, from enhancing floral designs to adorning gift-wrapped packages.

florist's bow: *round*

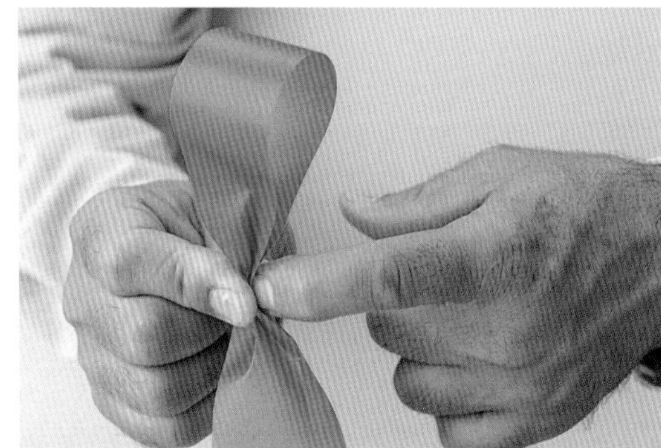

1) Form a loop with the ribbon, then crimp the ribbon tightly between your thumb and index finger. The size (length) of the loop should be equal to one half the size (diameter) of the completed bow.

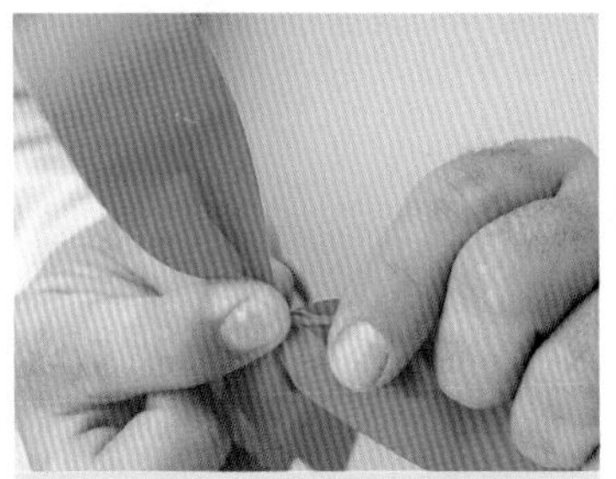

2) Twist the trailing length of ribbon at the crimp so that the finished side (if not using double-face ribbon) is facing outward (upward) while continuing to keep the center tightly crimped.

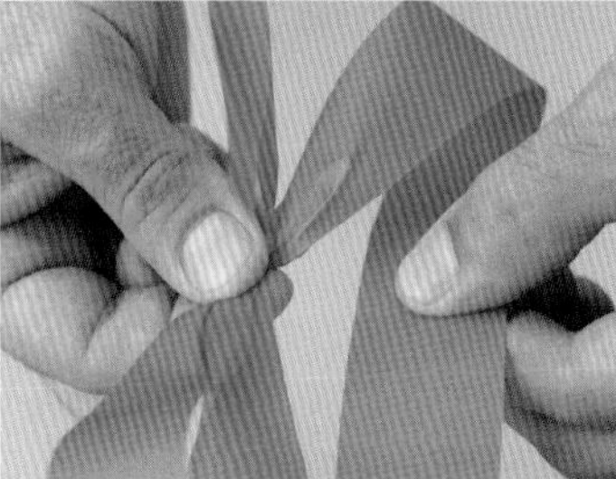

3) Form a second loop, opposite the first loop and equal in size, and crimp the ribbon between your thumb and index finger once again, gathering the ribbon under the initial crimp.

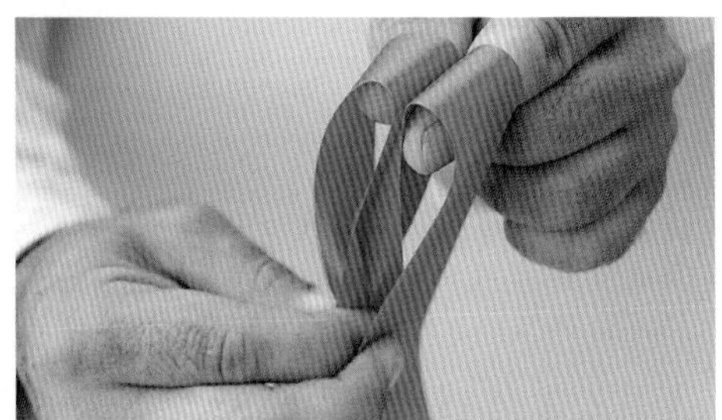

4) Continue creating equal-size loops, one on top of another, crimping and twisting the ribbon (Steps 1-3) until you reach the desired volume. Make sure to maintain a tight grip on the crimping in the center.

Note: Making all loops the same size will ensure that the bow will be symmetrical.

5) Tie a separate piece of ribbon over the center, and knot it securely in the back to hold the loops in place. You also can bind the ribbon with enameled florist's wire.

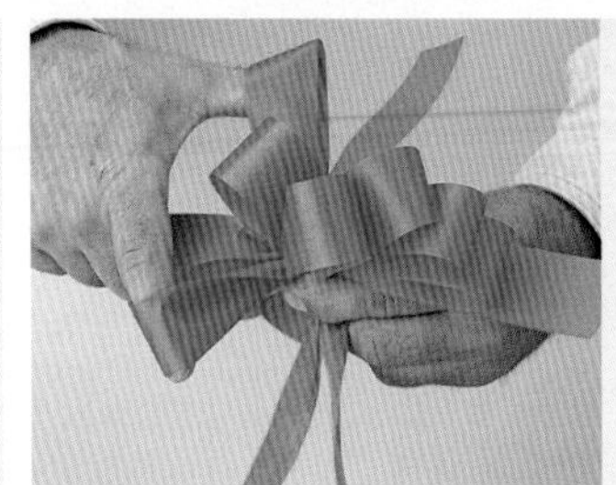

6) Shape the bow by pulling the loops from side to side, creating a symmetrical, well-formed bow.

florist's bow: *flat*

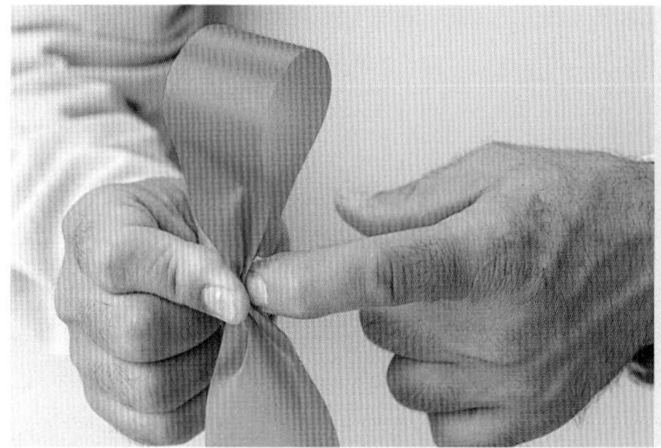

1) Form a loop with the ribbon, then crimp the ribbon tightly between your thumb and index finger. The size (length) of the loop should be equal to one half the size (diameter) of the completed bow.

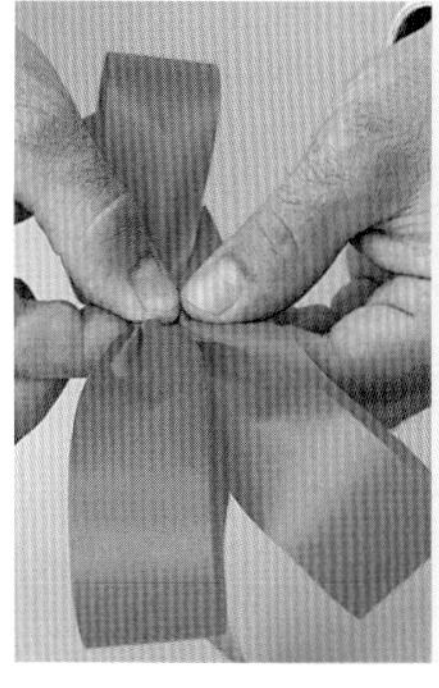

2) Twist the trailing length of ribbon at the crimp so that the finished side (if not using double-face ribbon) is facing outward (upward) while continuing to keep the center tightly crimped. Form a second loop, opposite the first loop and equal in size, and crimp the ribbon between your thumb and index finger once again, gathering the ribbon under the initial crimp.

3) Continue creating equal-size loops, crimping and twisting the ribbon (Steps 1 and 2) until you have formed the background of the bow. Position the ribbon as you make each loop so that the loops form the bow as you proceed. In this example, we show three loops on each side of the center.

4) Using the same techniques (Steps 1 and 2), make two additional loops on each side of the center, all equal size but smaller than the previously formed loops. These loops should be "stacked" on top of the first loops.

5) Complete the bow by forming a center loop: Bring the ribbon over your thumb, crimping it into the center. This loop will cover the center gathers.

6) Thread a length of enameled florist's wire through the center loop and over the center of the bow. Twist it tightly in the back of the bow. *Tip: Holding the wire and twisting the bow helps make the binding tighter and more secure.*

ribbon candy bow

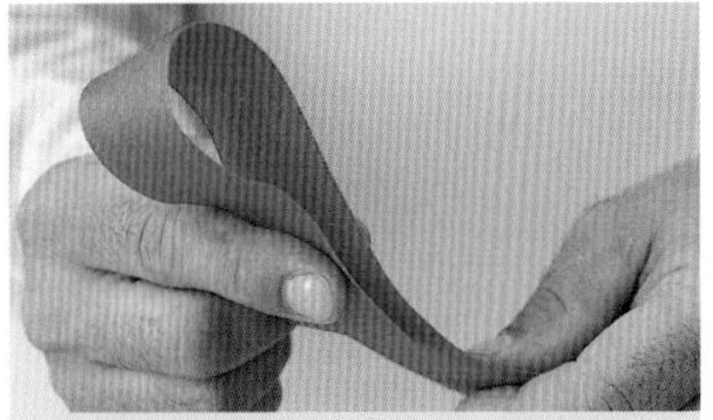

1) Create a loop with double-face ribbon, holding the ribbon flat between your thumb and index finger.

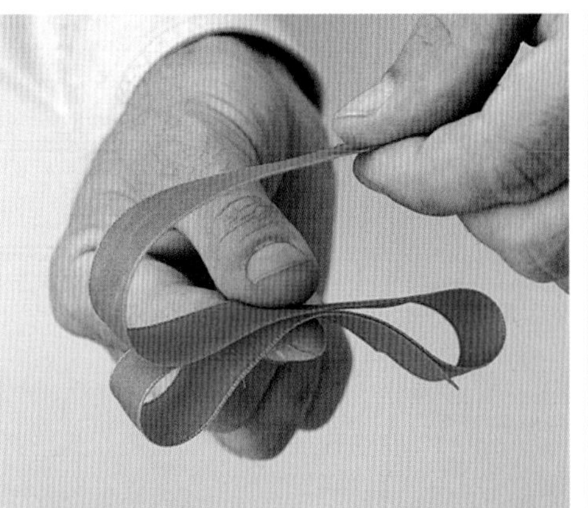

2) Make a second loop, in the opposite direction, on the opposite side of the center of the ribbon (where you are holding onto the ribbon). Continue making loops on both sides of the center, from one side to another, stacking layers of ribbon one on top of another, until you have the desired volume. Each pair of loops should be the same size, but each successive pair should be slightly smaller than the previous pair. Do not twist or crimp the ribbon in the center.

Optional: Make a final loop to go over your thumb, creating a nice finish.

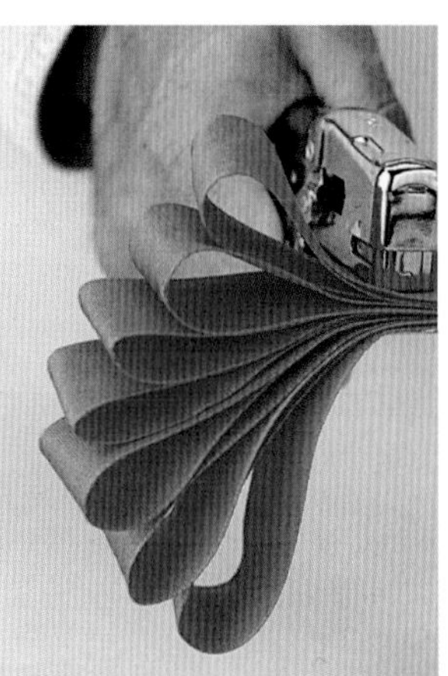

3) Staple the bow in the center.

pom-pom bow

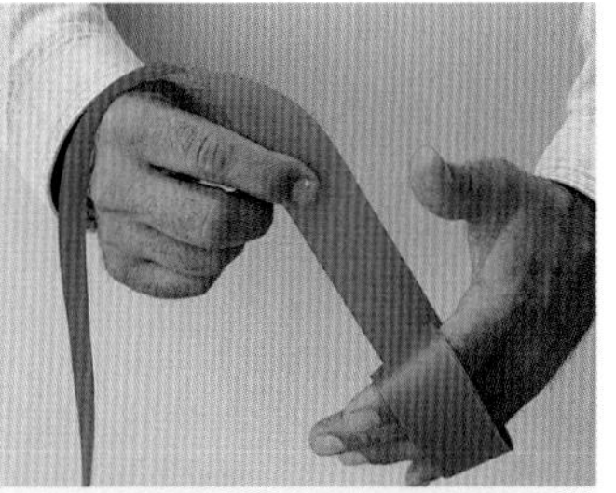

1) Wrap ribbon around your hand, with the finished side (if not using double-face ribbon) facing outward (upward), until you have the desired volume.

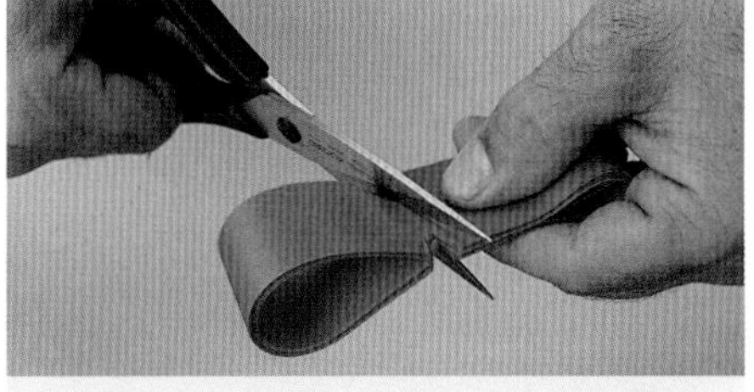

2) Slide the ribbon off your hand, keeping it together in a roll. Holding the roll of ribbon with one hand, flatten the center and cut notches in both edges of the center with sharp ribbon scissors. Hold the ribbon tightly enough to ensure that the center stays intact.

3) Tie a separate piece of ribbon through the notched area, and knot it tightly in the back.

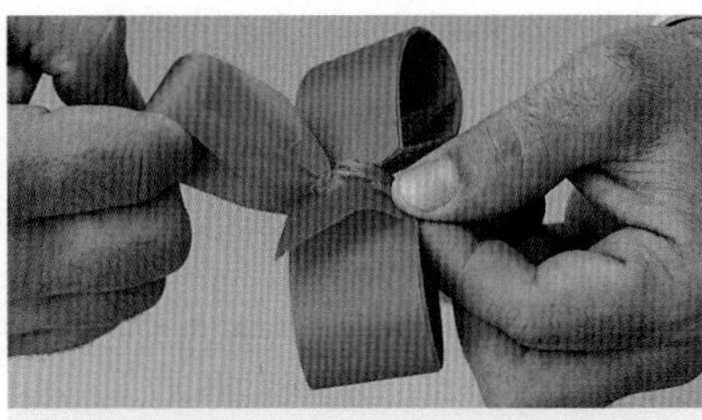

4) Begin pulling each loop away from the ribbon coil, and twisting each slightly to separate it and hold it in position.

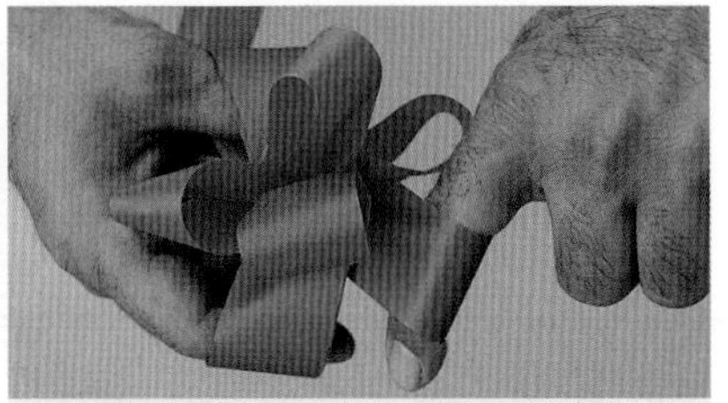

5) Continue pulling and twisting each loop until every loop is separated and in position and the bow is full.

dior bow

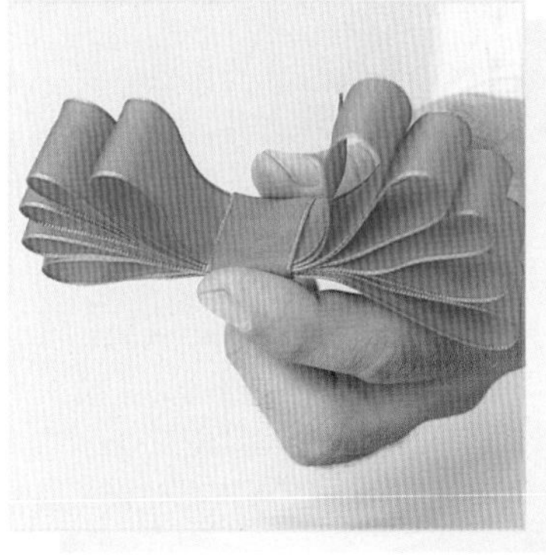

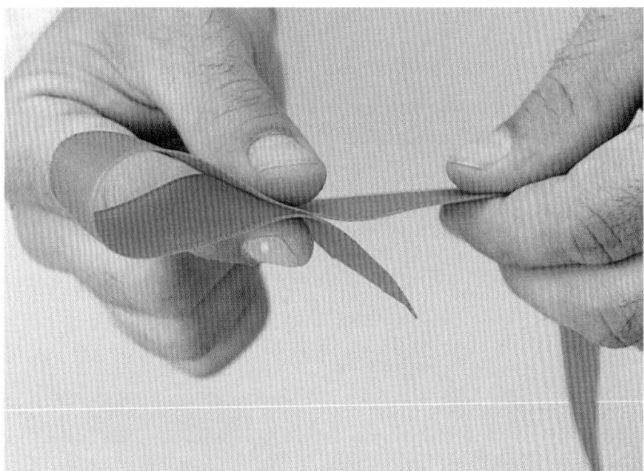

1) Create a loop with double-face ribbon, holding the ribbon flat between your thumb and index finger.

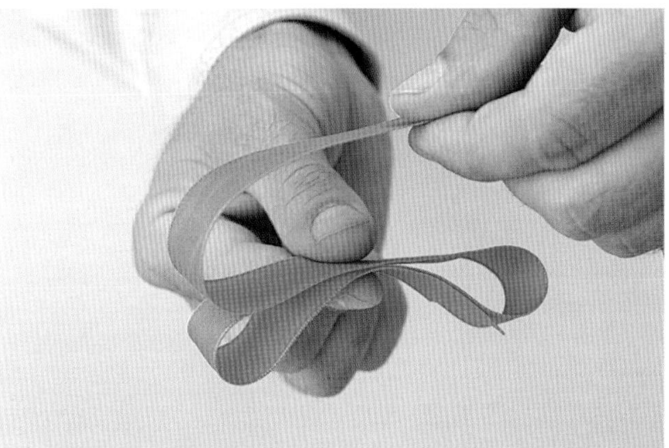

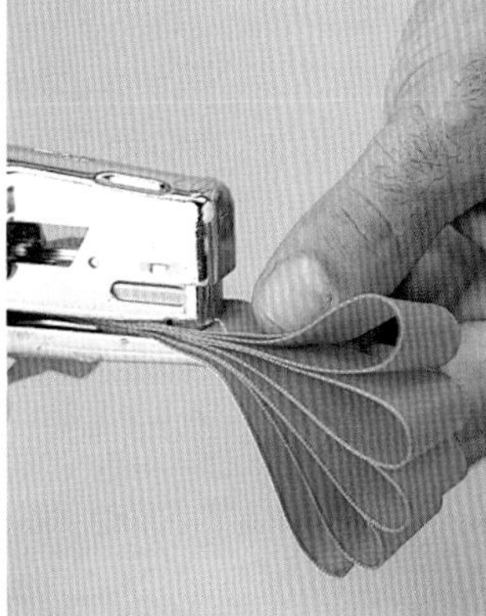

3) Staple the bow in the center.

2) Make a second loop, in the opposite direction, on the opposite side of the center of the ribbon (where you are holding onto the ribbon). Continue making loops on both sides of the center, from one side to another, stacking layers of ribbon one on top of another, until you have the desired volume. Each pair of loops should be the same size, but each successive pair should be slightly smaller than the previous pair. Do not twist or crimp the ribbon in the center.

Note: If using a single-face ribbon, each layer of loops will need to be created individually, then stacked one on top of another, and stapled together. This will maintain the finished side of the ribbon on the outside of each loop.

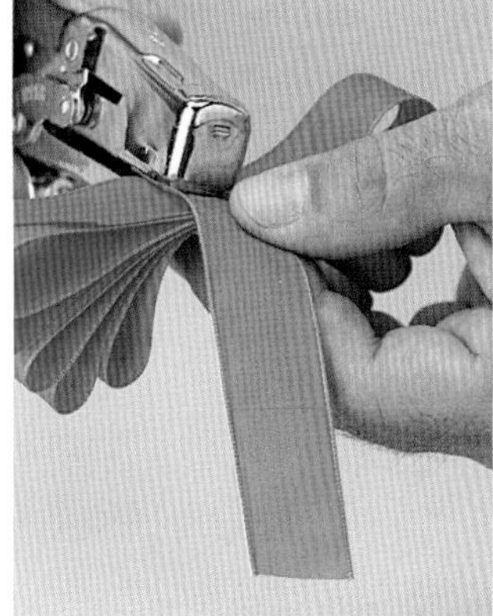

4) Staple a separate piece of ribbon to the back of the bow, in the center.

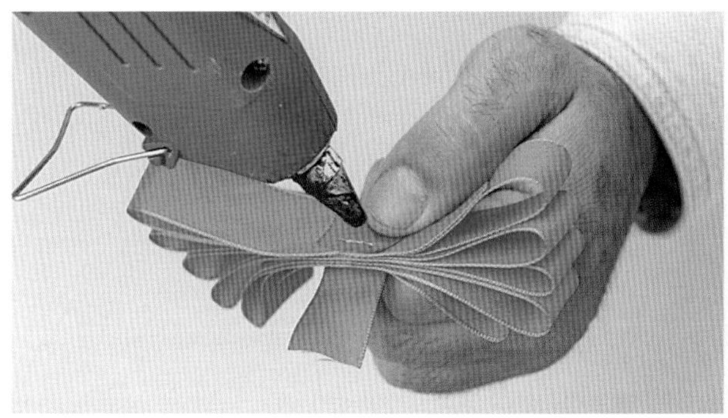

5) Bring that piece of ribbon over the front center of the bow, and return it to the backside of the bow, securing it in place with hot glue. This will cover the staple in the center of the bow and create the focal area of the bow.

index

8)
10)
12)
14)
16)
18)
20)
22)
24)
26)
28)
32)
34)
34)
34)
34)
36)
38)
40)
42)
44)
46)
46)
46)
46)
48)
50)
52)
56)
58)
60)
62)
64)
66)
68)
70)
72)
76)
78)
80)
82)
84)
86)
88)
90)
92)